Crosscurrents/MODERN CRITIQUES

Harry T. Moore, *General Editor*

Shadows of Imagination

The Fantasies of C. S. Lewis, J. R. R. Tolkien, and Charles Williams

EDITED BY

Mark R. Hillegas

WITH A PREFACE BY

Harry T. Moore

SOUTHERN ILLINOIS UNIVERSITY PRESS
Carbondale and Edwardsville

FEFFER & SIMONS, INC.
London and Amsterdam

Preface

Once upon a time—to begin fabulously—there was an editor of a series who had to write a preface for each of the books he chose for that series. This was not an easy task, but he did the best he could, often wishing that he had been born more glib. Since he read widely, however, he could generally manage to find something to say about whatever book he was dealing with. Then one day a manuscript came along which treated three authors he had not read with any thoroughness, nor did he intend to read them, although the book in question was one he had no hesitation in accepting. But how could he write a preface to this volume?

An even more pertinent question might be asked. Why, in the first place, did the editor select for his series a book about three authors he finds unreadable? The answer is that he doesn't find his preferences necessarily infallible. Ordinarily, he has convictions rather than opinions about literature; but the mere fact that he might find certain authors hard to read doesn't mean that they are poor writers, particularly when so many people whose judgment he respects happen to like those particular authors. And that is the answer.

This editor is aware that there are many other seasoned readers who, like him, cannot be fired up by C. S. Lewis, J. R. R. Tolkien, and Charles Williams (the editor admits that the only book by any of these fantasists which he read all the way through, Williams' All Hallows' Eve, he did enjoy). Like this editor, these other readers are not

all opposed to fantasy. As for himself, he grew up enjoy-
ing Gulliver's Travels and Alice in Wonderland, and he is
a deep admirer of Kafka. But he cannot become engrossed
by the whimsy of a Tolkien; let others enjoy it as much
as they please.

And he will help them along, and help the cause of
these three writers, by admitting the present book into the
Crosscurrents/Modern Critiques series. That series has
been fairly wide-ranging, and there is no reason why a
volume such as the present one should not be included.
So here it is, presented in the hope that it will please the
many intelligent readers interested in its material.

The editor's friend and colleague, Mark Hillegas, who
is himself the editor of this particular volume, follows this
Preface with an informative and persuasive Introduction
which makes out a good case for this special kind of
fantasy, showing how it has an appeal for many "literary
intellectuals," as Professor Hillegas designates them. He
tells how the present book originated in a special meeting
(the room was overcrowded) held during one of the
Modern Language Association conclaves a few years ago.

Although for reasons made clear in the foregoing I
cannot (as editor of this series) discuss the work of Lewis,
Tolkien, and Williams, I am pleased at least to help bring
before the academic reading public the expert comments
of the various authors in this book (one of them, J. B. S.
Haldane, appears in a negative capacity). I may add
that my associate in this enterprise, Mr. Vernon Sternberg,
Director of the Southern Illinois University Press, gave
his vote for the inclusion of this volume in the series,
though I'm not convinced that he reads Lewis, Tolkien,
and Williams avidly.

And now here is a list of those contributors, followed
by Mr. Hillegas' Introduction and the essays on the
fantasists.

HARRY T. MOORE

Southern Illinois University
March 2, 1969

Notes on Contributors

ALICE MARY HADFIELD, upon graduating from Oxford and then taking an M.A. from Mount Holyoke, became an assistant to Charles Williams at Oxford University Press at Amen House in London. Among her several books, she is the author of the first biography of Williams (*An Introduction to Charles Williams*, 1959). She is currently at work on a critical study of Williams' writings.

J. B. S. HALDANE, who died in 1964, is the world-famous biochemist, biologist, geneticist, Marxist, and philosopher and spokesman of science. He once remarked that the Christian account of the end of the universe suffered from two cardinal defects: it was written from the point of view of the angels and a small minority of the human race; and it grossly exaggerated the importance, in the scheme of the cosmos, of our planet and its inhabitants.

MARK R. HILLEGAS' area of scholarly specialization is the impact of science on literature, the relationship between the humanities and the sciences, and the literary imagination of science. He recently published *The Future as Nightmare: H. G. Wells and the Anti-Utopians* and since 1962 has taught, at both graduate and undergraduate levels, a course in science fiction and utopian fantasy. He is Associate Professor of English at Southern Illinois University.

DANIEL HUGHES is an Associate Professor at Wayne State University, specializing in English romanticism. His articles and reviews on Shelley, modern fiction, and poetry have appeared in *ELH*, *Studies in Romanticism*, the *Keats-Shelley Journal*,

Modern Fiction Studies, Massachusetts Review, and *The Nation.* His first book of poetry, *Waking in a Tree,* appeared in 1964, and a second is forthcoming.

W. R. IRWIN is the author of "There and Back Again: The Romances of Williams, Lewis, and Tolkien," which appeared in the *Sewanee Review* in 1961. The author of three books, he is currently completing a lengthy critical study of fantasy as a sub-genre in English and American fiction. He is Professor of English and Director of Graduate Study in English at the University of Iowa.

CLYDE S. KILBY, Professor of English at Wheaton College, was a personal friend of C. S. Lewis and spent the summer of 1966 working with J. R. R. Tolkien in Oxford. His several books include *The Christian World of C. S. Lewis* (1964); an edition of Lewis's correspondence, *Letters to an American Lady* (1967); and an anthology of Lewis's sayings and ideas, *A Mind Awake* (1968). He has lectured on Lewis and Tolkien at colleges and universities across the country.

CHARLES MOORMAN, author of six books and innumerable articles, is Professor of English and Associate Dean of the Graduate School at the University of Southern Mississippi. His most recent book is *A Knyght There Was: The Evolution of the Literary Knight* (1967); and his writings on the Oxford Christians include *Arthurian Triptych: Mythic Materials in Charles Williams, C. S. Lewis, and T. S. Eliot* (1960) and *The Precincts of Felicity: The Augustinian City of the Oxford Christians* (1966).

ROBERT PLANK, ACSW, is the author of *The Emotional Significance of Imaginary Beings* (1968). He is Program Chief, Social Work Service, Mental Hygiene Unit, Veterans Administration Hospital, Cleveland, Ohio, and Lecturer in English and Psychology, Case Western Reserve University.

PATRICIA MEYER SPACKS is Professor of English and Chairman of the Department at Wellesley College. Her many scholarly articles and books include *The Varied God: A Critical Study of Thomson's "The Seasons"* (1959), *The Insistence of Horror: Aspects of the Supernatural in Eighteenth-Century Poetry* (1962), and *The Poetry of Vision* (1967).

Her 1959 articles, "The Mythmaker's Dilemma: Three Novels by C. S. Lewis" (in *Discourse*) and "Ethical Patterns in *The Lord of the Rings*" (*Critique*), are well known to Lewis and Tolkien scholars.

GUNNAR URANG, Assistant Professor of English at Wooster College, has just completed his Ph.D. in Theology and Literature at the Divinity School of the University of Chicago, writing a dissertation on Lewis, Tolkien, and Williams. He recently contributed an essay to *Adversity and Grace: Recent Studies in American Literature* (1968), edited by Nathan A. Scott.

CHAD WALSH, poet, scholar, Episcopalian priest, and Professor of English at Beloit College, is well known for his many writings, which include *C. S. Lewis: Apostle to the Skeptics* (1949), *Campus Gods on Trial* (1953), and *From Utopia to Nightmare* (1962). His fifth book of poetry, *The End of Nature*, was published earlier this year.

GEORGE PARKER WINSHIP, JR., is Chairman of the Department of English at King College. He is the author of "This Rough Magic: The Novels of Charles Williams," an early, seminal article on Williams' fiction, which appeared in the *Yale Review* in 1950.

Contents

Preface   v

Notes on Contributors   vii

Introduction   xiii
    MARK R. HILLEGAS

C. S. Lewis   1

The Man and the Mystery
    CHAD WALSH

Auld Hornie, F.R.S.   15
    J. B. S. HALDANE

Some Psychological Aspects of Lewis's Trilogy   26
    ROBERT PLANK

Out of the Silent Planet as Cosmic Voyage   41
    MARK R. HILLEGAS

"Now Entertain Conjecture of a Time"–The
Fictive Worlds of C. S. Lewis and J. R. R.
Tolkien   59
    CHARLES MOORMAN

Meaning in The Lord of the Rings   70
    CLYDE S. KILBY

Pieties and Giant Forms in The Lord of the
Rings   81
    DANIEL HUGHES

Tolkien's Fantasy   97
The Phenomenology of Hope
    GUNNAR URANG

The Novels of Charles Williams   111
   GEORGE P. WINSHIP, JR.

The Relationship of Charles Williams' Working
Life to His Fiction   125
   ALICE MARY HADFIELD

Christian Doctrine and the Tactics of Romance   139
The Case of Charles Williams
   W. R. IRWIN

Charles Williams   150
The Fusions of Fiction
   PATRICIA MEYER SPACKS

Notes   160

Index   167

Introduction

The fantasies of C. S. Lewis, J. R. R. Tolkien, and
Charles Williams have a significance beyond their considerable intrinsic worth. A departure from the long-accepted
norms of realistic fiction, they offer an index to a major
shift in taste now under way. Another manifestation of
this shift is the post-realism of those whom Robert
Scholes calls the "fabulators" (writers like Murdoch, Nabokov, Barth), who also write a kind of fantasy. But
unlike the fabulators, Lewis, Tolkien, and Williams are
neither "comic allegorists" nor innovators in form and
verbal technique. In a sense the work of Lewis, Tolkien,
and Williams is a return to a mode of writing which has
been around for centuries but which, looked at one way,
fell from favor with the onset of "realism" in the nineteenth century, or, looked at another, declined in the
eighteenth century when the novel replaced the previously
dominant forms of the epic and romance. Lewis, Tolkien,
and Williams are closer to the *Odyssey*, *Divine Comedy*,
Paradise Lost, or *Faust* than they are to the fabulators.

Fantasy never died entirely, in spite of its rejection by a
majority of educated readers, writers, and critics. In the
twentieth century it has survived in works ranging from
the stories of Edgar Rice Burroughs or the lowest levels of
pulp science fiction to Kafka's *Metamorphosis* or the great
anti-utopias (Zamyatin's *We*, Huxley's *Brave New
World*, Orwell's *Nineteen Eighty-four*). Until recently,
though, the kind of fantasy usually written by Lewis,
Tolkien, and Williams (as distinguished from the *Robin-*

sonade and "rationalist" fantasy, such as utopias and anti-utopias) has been largely the exclusive property of a cult (the old *Weird Tales* was a major outlet, and the remarkable publisher, August Derleth, continues the tradition with Arkham House and books like Colin Wilson's recent *The Mind Parasites*). Occasionally this kind of fantasy achieved some sort of significance, as it did with the better stories of H. P. Lovecraft, E. R. Eddison's *The Worm Ouroboros*, David Lindsay's *A Voyage to Arcturus*, or Merwyn Peake's *Gormenghast Trilogy*. But with Lewis, Tolkien, and Williams we have it emerging, as it were, from the underground of the cultists.

Partly the emergence can be explained by the extraordinary seriousness with which Lewis, Tolkien, and Williams regard fantasy. They do not disdain it as mere "escape," Lewis and Williams agreeing with Tolkien in distinguishing between the "Flight of the Deserter" and the "Escape of the Prisoner." In their shared belief, it is a mode valuable for presenting moral or spiritual values, which could not be presented in realistic fiction: a way of transcending the limitations of human existence to attain new perspectives and insights. Such a similarity in viewpoint is not surprising when one remembers that they formed, with other friends, a group which met together twice weekly in Oxford during and after the war to talk and read works in progress. Thus Lewis read *Perelandra*, Williams *All Hallows' Eve*, and Tolkien (and later his son, Christopher) portions of *The Lord of the Rings*.

But chiefly the emergence of fantasy from the cultists' underground is due to the high order of excellence of what Lewis, Tolkien, and Williams have written, an excellence in turn dependent on their respect for fantasy. One would expect that in their writings there would be numerous parallels and, occasionally, direct indebtednesses, and indeed there are. Yet the interesting thing is that each writer is excellent in his own fashion, unique in style and technique. Lewis is, I think, the superior stylist of the group: his fantasies are written in an almost archetypally lucid, clear prose. His best work is the "cosmic trilogy" —

Out of the Silent Planet, Perelandra, That Hideous Strength—which I much prefer to his reworking of the Cupid and Psyche myth, *Till We Have Faces*, and his children's books, *The Chronicles of Narnia*. In the trilogy, he is at his most successful in "domesticating the incredible," in building a strong bridge from our real to his imaginary worlds, which are both solid and internally consistent. Over the years, of course, the trilogy changed as Lewis was writing it, moving from *Out of the Silent Planet* and something like Wells's *The First Men in the Moon* to finally, with *That Hideous Strength*, something more akin to Williams' "theological thrillers."

Charles Williams' fantastic novels are also linked to the real world, but Williams, much more than Lewis, blurs the distinction, and, indeed, as T. S. Eliot notes, there is no clear line of demarcation between natural and supernatural in them. Williams' style is murkier than Lewis's and his plots more sprawling. Unlike Lewis's novels, his might, with some accuracy, be called "tales of the weird and occult," varieties of the Gothic strain. They are quite good, but I suppose one would have to concede the rightness of judgment of many critics that they are inferior to his poetry.

Tolkien is still different, and further from Lewis and Williams than they are from each other. His *Lord of the Rings* is an extraordinary accomplishment in the writing of fantasy, for unlike most writers of successful fantasy, he uses no bridge to reality. To portray, as he does, an imaginary world without first leading us there from our own world is extremely difficult to do well, but this Tolkien has done, using only internal links: as Douglass Parker notes, chiefly the embodiment of human values and characteristics in the nonhuman world and the use of "archetypes of existent myths."

Aside from their excellence, the fantasies of these three men are of a sort which appeals especially to the literary community—"serious" novelists and poets, critics, professors of literature—whom one might call "literary intellectuals." Thus the enthusiastic response to the conference on the fiction of Lewis and Tolkien which was held at the annual meeting of the Modern Language Association in 1966 and which led to this volume. Thus the growing number of "academic" books and articles about these three writers. A useful way both to analyze the attraction for literary intellectuals of the fantasies of Lewis, Tolkien, and Williams and to understand better the nature of these writings is to compare them with another form of fantasy—science fiction—so important at a popular level in the twentieth century but which leaves most literary people cold.

One has to admit that one reason why literary intellectuals find science fiction unpalatable is that much of it is badly written: crude in construction and infelicitous in style. But, as Kingsley Amis makes clear in *New Maps of Hell*, this is not always true, and, in fact, a good deal of it is quite interesting and important (though certainly a very different thing from regular fiction). But literary people usually do not like even good science fiction, and for this there is a very sound reason: the *Weltanschauung* of most writers of science fiction.

I think there are two aspects of this problem. First, most literary intellectuals are hostile to the quantifying, materialistic vision of the universe and human existence which, as C. C. Gillispie reminds us, is that of science and, therefore, we can conclude, that of most science fiction, which has usually been written by people with technical or scientific education. Many literary intellectuals are like the earlier romantics, reacting "against a measuring, numbering science which alienates the creator of science from his own creation by total objectification of nature." They wish that science had never begun the process of taking mind out of the universe, and although the Christian mythology now seems dead to great numbers of them, they long for some myth to bring meaning again to the universe and human existence. And, of course, some like Eliot have managed to hang on to the Christian myth. Our three writers are in this latter category (the fantasies of Lewis and Williams are overtly

Christian and, although Tolkien's are probably not, his Christian faith is implicit). It is not hard to understand the appeal of their fantasies, in which the universe is alive with meaning.

The second aspect of the problem of the values of science-fiction writers—and here again we can make a useful comparison with the fantasies of Lewis, Tolkien, and Williams—is that science fiction is the myth of machine civilization, which, in its utopian extrapolation, it tends to glorify. It hardly needs saying that literary intellectuals are rather nauseated by machine civilization. Partly, I think, this response is related to their attitudes towards science, but largely it is because they are heirs to the horror and shock felt by so many nineteenth-century writers and other sensitive people at the new industrialism and commercialism. It was an enormous transformation —at times cruel and unjust and ugly—which not only changed the face of the land and the conditions of human life but also the very fabric of the social order, and literary intellectuals have never adjusted to it. Their continued resentment is overt in the fantasies of Lewis and Williams and just below the surface in Tolkien.

Finally, one can summarize not only the attitudes of Lewis, Tolkien, and Williams to science and machine civilization but also their philosophical-theological underpinning by pointing out that they belong to the broad cultural movement which, gaining momentum in the twenties and thirties, turned from dreams of reason, progress, science and the perfectibility of man to tradition and the doctrine of original sin. Lewis, Tolkien, and Williams are very much a part of this movement and, particularly in the case of Lewis and Williams, very close to Eliot, the symbolic father of it all.

One wonders, in this new era of post-realism, what Lewis, Tolkien, and Williams portend for the future. I think there will be a good number of imitations of their work, particularly Tolkien's, but lacking, as imitations usually do, the vitality of the originals. At the same time, there should be a revival of interest in such lesser works, already in existence, as *The Worm Ouroboros* or the *Gormenghast Trilogy.*

But what of the time when the cultural movement to which Lewis, Tolkien, and Williams belong has broken up, as I think it already shows signs of doing? (One sign is the weakening of the opposition to scientific utopianism.) Projecting the two trends—the swing from realism and the end of the antirationalist movement—we might speculate that we will eventually see fantasy of major importance presenting what Lewis has called the ideas of the "other side." It would be something like science fiction, but more substantial than anything yet written in this form. And as in the Hegelian dialectic of *thesis, antithesis,* and *synthesis,* the writers of this new fantasy will have learned something, at least about writing fantasy, from Lewis, Tolkien, and Williams.

A word about this book. It had its inception, as I have indicated, at an MLA Conference in 1966 on the fiction of Lewis and Tolkien. (Limitations of time dictated that Williams be omitted from formal discussion, though he was often mentioned.) The Conference was unusually successful: the room was packed, with people standing at the back and overflowing into the hall, and the give-and-take between audience and panel was extraordinarily lively. Indeed, the response was so enthusiastic that it seemed worthwhile to carry the discussion over into a book.

In preparing this volume, I have included essays by three of the original panelists (W. R. Irwin, Clyde S. Kilby, and Charles Moorman) as well as essays by others who were not participants. With two exceptions, none of the material has ever appeared in print before. The first exception is Chad Walsh's essay, which in a different form was published under the title "The Elusively Solid C. S. Lewis" in *Good Work* (Winter, 1967). I wish to thank the editor, Christopher Derrick, for permission to use it here. The other exception is J. B. S. Haldane's "Auld Hornie, F.R.S." Lewis and Haldane were, on intellectual and philosophical grounds, bitterly opposed, and I have included Haldane's critique of the "cosmic trilogy" as a representation of the views of the "other side." It first appeared in *The Modern Quarterly* (Autumn, 1946); and for permission to reprint it, I am grateful to George Allen & Unwin, Ltd., publishers of Haldane's *Everything Has a History*, in which it was later published.

Haldane's perspective is, of course, balanced by the essays of several Christian humanists. The principle of selection in putting together this volume has been to achieve as much variety in approach and viewpoint as possible: not only the biologist and Marxist, Haldane, but an expert in psychological analysis, two poets, and various scholar-critics have their say.

For permission to use the quotation from J. R. R. Tolkien's *The Lord of the Rings* in the essay by Daniel Hughes, I wish to thank the publishers George Allen & Unwin, Ltd. and Houghton Mifflin Company.

Carbondale, Illinois   MARK R. HILLEGAS
December 18, 1968

Shadows of Imagination

C. S. Lewis
The Man and the Mystery

CHAD WALSH

The mystery of C. S. Lewis is that there seems to be no mystery. None, at least, if one views the man through his books. No writer in our times has been more blessed with the gift of clarity. He could take the tangled doctrine of the Trinity and expound it in such a way that the curious atheist at least grasped what his Christian neighbors were fussing about. His literary criticism—a field in which turgid and tortured prose abounds—was crisp, to the point, never ambiguous. Even his most imaginative works, which roam through acres of mythology—the interplanetary novels, *Till We Have Faces*, the Narnia books, for instance—do not operate in a shimmering Celtic twilight. Though one has never met a *hross* or a *sorn*, a space-traveler to Mars would recognize them instantly, and would have a useful knowledge of how to communicate with them.

Nor did personal acquaintance with the man change the impression of an overwhelming clarity. I suppose I knew him as well as all but a handful of Americans. I was haunted by the sense of being with someone whose public image and private reality were identical—and somehow I was unwilling to believe that this can be true of any writer. I suppose I was influenced by the "spirit of the time," the basically psychological bias of modern thought. I went probing for the complexes, the secrets of the Id, and I seemed to find nothing. I did not feel that Lewis was concealing anything, but simply that there was nothing to conceal. Was it possible that he was simply what

1

his books suggested that he was, and that the inner man and the public man were one?

Two recent books provide some posthumous help at this point. *Light on C. S. Lewis* [1]—written by nine authors, all but one of whom knew him personally—poses exactly the same question. But for the moment, the companion book, *Letters of C. S. Lewis*,[2] would seem to offer more direct light. Here is a fat volume of letters, beginning shortly before Lewis's seventeenth birthday and continuing almost to the week of his death.

As a bonus, Lewis's slightly older brother, Major W. H. Lewis, contributes an admirable biographical memoir which spells out certain details that are not well covered in *Surprised by Joy*—for instance, Lewis's relation with his "mother," the lady he took into his home after her son, a friend of his, was killed in World War I. Major Lewis suggests that her tyrannical and anti-intellectual temperament was a sore burden to the good Samaritan who housed her. Here too is a luminous description of the remarkable woman whom Lewis eventually married, Joy Davidman Gresham.

The letters themselves are a literary delight from beginning to end. But the reader soon discovers that it is almost as though he is reading fragments of previously unpublished books. The letters are so much of the same tone and content as the familiar Lewis works that they give little new insight into Lewis. Apparently the "real Lewis" is the one his readers have known all along.

Often the letters foreshadow the books, even in trivial details. In *That Hideous Strength* (1945) the young sociologist nervously cuts himself while shaving, and is self-consciously aware of the blemish when he goes to his interview with the chiefs of the N.I.C.E. But twenty-four years earlier, in a letter to his brother, Lewis had written of a ceremonious occasion at Oxford, when undergraduates one by one are the public targets of homilies delivered by the Master.

> I doubt if even our father could have invented anything more subtly undermining of one's self-respect. . . . Try to

imagine it, and then add the idea of 9 in the morning; and that your collar has broken loose from its stud at the back; and that there is a smell of last night's dinner about it; a fly on your nose; a shaving cut beginning to bleed—but no, it is too painful. (p. 55)

The same young sociologist was consumed with yearning to be an "insider" at the N.I.C.E., and the theme of "insiders" is developed by Lewis in one of his most trenchant essays, "The Inner Ring" (published in *Transposition and Other Addresses*, 1949). But in 1921 it was Lewis who gazed at an inner ring, and felt acutely he was on the outside:

> The real Oxford is a close corporation of the jolly, untidy, lazy, good-for-nothing, humorous old men, who have been electing their own successors ever since the world began and who intend to go on with it. They'll squeeze under the Revolution or leap over it when the time comes, don't you worry. When I think how little chance I have of ever fighting my way into that unassuming but impregnable fortress, that modest unremoveability, that provoking intangible stone wall, I think of Keats's poison
> > Brewed in monkish cell
> > to thin the scarlet conclave of old men. (p. 60)

The reader looking for the key influences in Lewis's life will find them in the letters, but they are already presented and analyzed with equal candor (and equal reticence) in the autobiography, *Surprised by Joy*. Letters and autobiography alike give the same curious impression: of telling all up to a certain point, and then drawing a curtain so that one does not know whether that *is* all, or whether the real mystery and secret are now hidden behind the veil of some private temple.

The two strands that run through C. S. Lewis's books are "logic" and "romance," to give them the names he chose. Jointly they led him back to Christianity. Both are evident early in the letters. In a letter to his father, written in 1921, he laments the death of "Old Kirk," who had been his private tutor:

What shall one say of him? It would be a poor compliment to that memory to be sentimental; indeed if it were possible, he himself would return to chide the absurdity. It is however no sentiment but plainest fact to say that I owe him in the intellectual sphere as much as one human being can owe another. . . . It was an atmosphere of unrelenting clearness and rigid honesty of thought that one breathed from living with him—and this I shall be the better for as long as I live. (pp. 53–54)

But only two years later (while still far from a Christian commitment) we find him speaking of George Macdonald, whose benign spirit was to be his Beatrice in *The Great Divorce*:

After this I read Macdonald's *Phantastes* over my tea, which I have read many times and which I really believe fills for me the place of a devotional book. (p. 84)

It was the combination of Old Kirk's logic and Macdonald's transcendent intuitions that shaped the mature sensibility of Lewis and gave to his books their peculiar and powerful simultaneous appeal to mind and heart. Or to put it with more accuracy, these two men—one in the flesh and the other from the printed page—made him recognize the two sides of his nature that were already latent.

The letters do amplify in interesting ways the impression that Lewis's readers—both friendly and hostile—have always had: that he was out of joint with the times. He set himself against the most fashionable intellectual currents, and rather gloried in the role, as witness his famous "dinosaur address" when he was inaugurated as a professor at Cambridge. For a long time, in his young manhood, he staked his main hopes on being a poet, but with an acute awareness that he was unfashionable. In 1920, we find him involved in putting together an anthology

as a kind of counterblast to the ruling literary fashion here, which consists in the tendencies called "Vorticist." Vorticist poems are usually in "vers libre" (which means that they are printed like verse, but neither rhyme nor scan, a line ending wherever you like). Some of them are clever, the majority merely affected, and a good few—especially among the French ones—indecent; not a sensuous indecency but one meant to nauseate, the whole genus arising from the "sick of everything" mood. So some of us others who are not yet sick of everything, have decided to bring out a yearly collection of our own things in the hope of persuading the gilded youth that the possibilities of metrical poetry on sane subjects are not yet quite exhausted. (pp. 51–52)

Much of the later Lewis is already there: the reaction against modish modernism, a sensibility that was *not* "sick of everything," the loving use of the word "sane."

If the twentieth century is permeated and dominated by psychology, so that many novels are little more than slightly dramatized monologues straight from the Freudian couch, Lewis will have none of it. In 1927, in a letter to his father, he mentioned that he had been reading *The Woman in White* and added:

Of course only third-rate people write that sort of novel now, whereas Wilkie Collins was clearly a man of genius; and there is a good deal to be said for his point of view (expressed in the preface) that the first business of a novel is to tell a story and that characters etc. come second. (p. 121)

His impatience with much modern literature is bluntly stated in a letter to Ruth Pitter (1951):

What is the point of keeping in touch with the contemporary scene? Why shd. one read authors one doesn't like because they happen to be alive at the same time as oneself? One might as well read everyone who had the same job or the same coloured hair or the same income or the same chest measurement, so far as I can see. (pp. 225–26)

Lewis's antimodernism had its unpleasant side. He could be too quick to assume that the new and unfamiliar was somehow allied with the powers of darkness. Take the case of Teilhard de Chardin, the Jesuit scholar whose major works were suppressed by his order during his lifetime, but who now shows signs of being the nearest thing to a twentieth-century Thomas Aquinas. There is an impatient superficiality in Lewis's letter to Father Peter Milward (1960):

> I am entirely on the side of your society for shutting de Chardin up. The enormous boosts he is getting from scientists who are very hostile to you seem to me v. like the immense popularity of Pasternak among anti-Communists. I can't for the life of me see his merit. The cause of Man against men never needed championing *less* than now. There seems to me a dangerous (but also commonplace) tendency to Monism or even Pantheism in this thought. And what in Heaven's name is the sense of saying that before there was life there was "pre-life"? If you choose to say that before you switched on the light in the cellar there was "pre-light," of course you may. But the ordinary English word of "pre-light" is darkness. What do you gain by such nicknames? (p. 296)

This is "Old Kirk's" logic-chopping carried to a point where it renders Lewis blind to the possibility that Chardin was attempting, for our times, a new synthesis of faith and secular knowledge. It points also to what was both a strength and a limitation in Lewis's religious thought—its predominantly static quality. He defended that faith once and for all delivered to the saints, and expected those paid soldiers of the faith, the clergy, to do likewise. He showed too little awareness of the possibility that new light might somehow blaze from and on the Gospel, and that men who apparently were flirting with heresy might be the pathfinders to a deeper understanding.

At least the logical Lewis, the spiritual child of Old Kirk, suffered from this limitation. The Lewis begotten of George Macdonald—the poetic, intuitive Lewis—had his moments when he realized the mysterious and devious ways in which God reveals himself. In a letter to his brother (1932) he almost develops a theory of multiple revelation, but draws back at the last minute:

Sometimes, relying on Christ's remark, "other sheep have I that are not of this fold" I have played with the idea that Christianity was never intended for Asia—even that Buddha is the form in which Christ appears to the Eastern mind. (p. 152)

The hesitation quickly ends and he briskly adds, "But I don't think this will really work." In the final book of the Narnia series he comes at the question in another way, when the noble worshipper of a pagan god discovers in the moment of apocalyptic revelation that all along he has actually worshipped Aslan the divine lion without knowing the real name. In general, however, Lewis is much more concerned to build a fortress around the traditional core of Christian dogma and to invite one and all inside the redoubt, than to explore odd and perilous byways of religious truth.

This brief foray into the *Letters* leads naturally to *Light on C. S. Lewis*, a remarkably interesting composite book, with individual chapters by a cross section of his friends and admirers. The essays are prefaced by Owen Barfield's splendid Introduction, in which he draws together clues from the other authors and attempts to prove the mystery of Lewis's seeming lack of mystery. A lifelong friend of Lewis from undergraduate days, Barfield is in a peculiarly strategic position to clarify the question of "the real Lewis."

John Lawlor—a pupil of Lewis's, now a professor of English at the University of Keele—confirms the impression I had when I first met Lewis:

One quickly felt that for him dialectic supplied the place of conversation. Any general remarks were of an obvious and even platitudinous kind; talk was dead timber until the spark of argument flashed. Then in a trice you were whisked from the particular to fundamental principles; thence (if you wanted) to eternal verities; and Lewis was alert for any riposte you could muster. . . . He was, of course, only passing on what he had learned from "the Great Knock" ["Old Kirk"]. . . . He was the dialectician all his life; and one must only add that he was superb. (pp. 67–68)

His Oxford colleague and friend, Professor Nevill Coghill, singles out another trait that may be closely related to the above:

> Underneath all, I sense in his style an indefeasible core of Protestant certainties, the certainties of a simple, unchanging, entrenched ethic that knows how to distinguish, unarguably, between Right and Wrong, Natural and Unnatural, High and Low, Black and White, with a committed force, an ethic on which his ramified and seemingly conciliatory structures of argument are invisibly based; but the strength that they derive from this hard core deprived him of certain kinds of sympathy and perception. (p. 60)

It is, however, to Owen Barfield's Introduction that I turn for the most convincing light on Lewis. Barfield records his growing bewilderment during the 1930's when it seemed to him that some kind of change was taking place in Lewis, an alteration not necessarily connected with the conversion from theism to Christianity which had just occurred. (I might add parenthetically that the *Letters* do not suggest any marked change in the man during the 1930's; at most an intensification of the traits that were already there.) It began when Barfield read Lewis's *Open Letter to Tillyard* and came to its elegantly courteous conclusion:

> We have both learnt our dialectic in the rough academic arena where knocks that would frighten the London literary coteries are given and taken in good part; and even where you may think me something too pert you will not suspect me of malice. If you honour me with a reply it will be in kind; and then, God defend the right!
>   I am, my dear Sir, with the greatest respect,
>
>   Your obedient servant,
>   C. S. Lewis (p. x)

Barfield tells how he slapped down the article and shouted: "I don't believe it! It's pastiche!" This little episode led him to sense a mystery in Lewis—a curious impersonality, an unwillingness to explore the inner self, the creation of a personality turned outward for public debate. He asks:

> *Was* there something, at least in his impressive, indeed splendid, literary personality, which was somehow—and with no taint of insincerity—*voulu*? So that, taken in conjunction with his immersion in the literature of the past and his imaginative power of vigorously re-animating it, there was something that would justify my involuntary exclamation . . . some touch of more than merely *ad hoc* pastiche? (p. xi)

Barfield then moves to a theory that, more than any other statement I have seen, clarifies the nature of Lewis's writings and the mystery (or lack of mystery!) in the man himself:

> If it is true that Lewis was not much interested in depth-psychology, it is not true that he had never thought about it. As a young man, for instance, he had been quite aware of the technique of diagnosing the psyche in terms of its latent perversion—and quite capable of applying this technique to himself, and incidentally to me. What I think is true is, that at a certain stage in his life he deliberately ceased to take any interest in himself except as a kind of spiritual alumnus taking his moral finals. I think this was part of the change to which I have referred; and I suggest that what began as deliberate choice became at length (as he had no doubt always intended it should) an ingrained and effortless habit of soul. Self-knowledge, for him, had come to mean recognition of his own weaknesses and shortcomings and nothing more. Anything beyond that he sharply suspected, both in himself and in others, as a symptom of spiritual megalomania. At best, there was so much else in letters and in life, that he found much *more* interesting! (p. xvi)

I think Barfield has the clue. The twentieth century is overwhelmingly psychological in its way of thinking and feeling—at least this is true of Western Europe and the United States. Lewis, perhaps deliberately, set himself in opposition. He decided, consciously or intuitively, that

God's total creation is considerably more interesting and important than the turgid and elusive depths of the psyche, and that he would look outward rather than inward.

This statement of course requires many qualifications. Lewis had, for one thing, a peculiarly penetrating insight into man's moral life, the capacity for self-perception and rationalization. But what he did not choose to probe was the Freudian depths (though Barfield assures us that he had the usual layman's familiarity with Freud). Nor did he go on reductionist expeditions to find "the real self" —his own or others'—a quest often like peeling one onion skin after another in the hope of finding at last the "real onion." I think he took his own self as a "given," decided to live with it, and devote his attention to work, other people, God and God's total world. Duty became a more important word than self-knowledge.

Who is to say he made the wrong decision? As a college professor, I have observed the increasing psychologization of American students, their desperate efforts to find "the authentic self," their frantic fascination with existentialism (not its action-aspects so much as those phases that emphasize the solitary self), and recently the interest in psychedelic drugs as a means of exploring states of consciousness. With most of them it seems the pursuit of a will-o'-the-wisp. The "authentic self" always moves one step farther away with each desperate lunge toward it. Meanwhile, the outer world—other people, jobs to do, injustices to be righted, possibly God to know, rocks and trees and quasars—is waiting to be examined, explored, even glorified. Lewis felt himself part of a universe he had not created; his task was not to explore his own psyche but to relate himself to the totality of which he was a part. His tools for this were a sharp mind honed razor-keen by Old Kirk, aided by an intuitive awareness of the magical reality that breaks through into the everyday world at uncovenanted moments, and most of all the conviction that in the Christian faith there is available the essential things one needs to know in order to be a proper part of the totality.

Lewis paid a price. His literary judgments, like those of the Dr. Johnson whom he resembles in so many ways, are sometimes too rational, too clear-cut. He can hack his way through acres of critical nonsense, but in the process he tramps down certain interesting and important little growths of insight. His religious thinking is strong on the "either-or" challenge of the Christian faith, but edged at times with too shrill and simple a moralism, and inadequate awareness of the paradoxes of the Christian life and the ways in which God often works through those who apparently least succeed in living by the rulebook. Lewis creates vivid and believable characters in his stories, but they are always mysterious in the same way that Lewis is: after he presents them to a certain depth, the curtain descends, and the reader is not sure whether anything exists behind.

He was not a Dostoevsky, either as a fiction writer or as a religious thinker. Or to make a couple of comparisons closer to his intentions, he was not a George Macdonald or a Charles Williams, though both of these men profoundly influenced him. It is difficult to put into words what the difference is, but any sensitive reader can immediately sense it. Lewis's novels have clarity and clean edges. There is a tender vagueness to the writing of Macdonald and Williams, a shimmering ambiguity, a haunting hint that God's ways are always half veiled and that in his dealings with humans we see only the part of the iceberg above the waters of the boundless ocean; in these two writers there is also an understanding of the mysteries of love—human and divine—and its paradoxes that Lewis never fully achieved. The Christian universe of his two mentors is open-ended, open-sided in a way that Lewis's is not.

If Lewis had lived longer, I think he might have explored more deeply the mysteries of the self. His final and most haunting novel, *Till We Have Faces* (1956), is his most psychological, and marks a considerable advance in his understanding of love. A year later he married Joy Davidman Gresham, and this supremely happy marriage affected his writing for the good. No one can read *The Four Loves* (1960) and compare it with his earlier treatments of marriage and love, and not sense a new depth and a franker awareness of how the sensual heart and body have their rights, not purely rational but going beyond mere rationality.

But of all his books the one that shows the greatest advance in human (and perhaps divine?) depth is *A Grief Observed*, published in 1961 under the pseudonym of N. W. Clerk. This is the raw cry of agony, a series of notebooks he kept after Joy's death, when his world collapsed about him, and all the tidy assurances of God's reality seemed a child's household of cardboard playthings. Here is a Lewis plunged into the depths of a Job, stripped of all that had given him assurance, compelled to live day by day in the darkness of utter bereavement. When he comes up at last into the sunlight and rediscovers, in a convincing but still tentative way, the presence of God, the discovery carries more conviction to the reader than the neatly marshalled ranks of arguments in *Mere Christianity* or even the glowing Christian mythology of the interplanetary novels and Narnia tales.

Death took him too soon. After the loss of Joy, his health declined rapidly. When I last saw him at his home on the outskirts of Oxford late in 1961, he was subdued, elegiac; I think he had lost the will to live, and that death was a friend whom he would not deliberately seek, but would welcome when the visitor came. There was neither time nor energy left to go on from the discoveries that life had compelled him to make in his own self. If he could have lived another ten years in good health, who can say? He already had one of the most formidably clear Christian minds of the century. He had an imagination that could make "romance," the sudden moments of intuition and insight, gleam with the brightness of burnished myth. He had lacked only that something more which can be given only by those who have undertaken a journey to the end of the night within the self and returned to share the knowledge.

He died. The same day that President Kennedy was felled by a bullet, Lewis died quietly of a heart attack. It is futile to lament the books he did not write. Rather, give thanks for the generous and varied harvest of one life. Much of his literary criticism, such as *The Allegory of Love*, is already so standard that any scholar in the same field must begin where Lewis left off. His popularized treatments of Christianity—*Mere Christianity*, most of all —have given thousands their first coherent understanding of the rudiments of the faith. They may seem too tidy, too moralistic, but they draw the map of faith in bold strokes, and leave it for others to add the fine details and propose modifications.

His greatest legacy to us is, however, those books in which his soaring imagination, fed by what he calls "romance," created whole worlds mythologically alive. No one can read the interplanetary novels and henceforth think of space as mere "empty space"; in the act of reading, space becomes golden with the divine presence. The Narnia books incarnate the Christian vision in fairy tale form. *Till We Have Faces* has a complexity and obscurity that render it more akin to the intractably "modern" literature of our times than anything else Lewis did, and it continues to yield meaning after meaning on rereading. *The Great Divorce* makes the decisions between heaven and hell inescapably and imaginatively real. Finally, Lewis's "de profundis," *A Grief Observed*, is in its tortured but ultimately triumphant way one of the great devotional books of our times.

One concluding thought. Lewis's very limitation is, in a way, a great bounty. In the twentieth century the writers have been pathfinders in an increasing subjectivity, so that the novel today more often consists of clashing thoughts and inner emotions than of deeds that a movie camera could record. The general public, at least the more literate, has moved in the same direction. Many strands of theology are equally subjective. To the profound subjectivist, Lewis stands in unyielding opposition. Here is a superbly intelligent man, blessed with a literary gift of very high order, who presents a world that is what it is because God made it, and will continue to be what it is after any individual is no longer among those present. And furthermore, here is Lewis saying, in effect, that this is fine; God's universe is a more interesting object of study and field of action than the individual's psyche. This challenge will seem appallingly superficial to the convinced subjectivist; he will return to his analyst, his treatises on existentialism, his LSD. But he will have been challenged. And such are the vagaries of fashion—even fashions in moods and sensibilities—that it is not possible to extrapolate a trend into the future and say it will accelerate forever. Quite possibly, at some time that no one can predict, the Ego-searching and the Id-probing of our times will lose its fascination, and men will suddenly see an interesting world outside themselves, a world with which they can enter into significant relations. With a sigh of relief, they may turn from the ever-receding self to the non-self, and in joyfully accepting it, know themselves at last.

If this happens, Lewis may serve as a spiritual mentor for many of them. He is the specialized guide through a world that he did not create, the world that is simply there because God put it there.

Auld Hornie, F.R.S.

J. B. S. HALDANE

Mr. C. S. Lewis is a prolific writer of books which are intended to defend Christianity. Some of these are cast in the form of fiction. The most interesting group is perhaps a trilogy describing the adventures of Mr. Ransom, a Cambridge teacher of philology. In the first volume Ransom is kidnapped by a physicist called Weston and his accomplice, Divine, and taken in a "spaceship" to the planet Mars, which is inhabited by three species of fairly intelligent and highly virtuous and healthy vertebrates ruled by an angel. Weston wants to colonise the planet, and Divine to use it as a source of gold. Their efforts are frustrated, and they return to earth, bringing Ransom with them.

In the second volume the angel in charge of Mars takes Ransom to Venus, where he meets the Eve of a new human race, which has just been issued with souls. Weston also arrives, allows the devil to possess him, and acts as serpent in a temptation of the new Eve. Ransom's arguments against the devil are inadequate, so he finally kills Weston, and is returned to earth by angels, with thanks for services rendered.

In the final book two still more sinister scientists, Frost and Wither, who have given their souls to the devil, are running the National Institute of Co-ordinated Experiments. Devine, now a peer, is helping them. The only experiment described is the perfusion of a severed human head, through which the devil issues his commands. They are also hoping to resurrect Merlin, who has been asleep for fifteen centuries in their neighbourhood. Their aim appears to be the acquisition of superhuman power and of immortality; though how this is to be done is far from clear, just as it is far from clear why a severed head perfused with blood should live longer than a normal one, or be a more suitable instrument for the devil. However, Mr. Ransom is too much for them. He obtains the assistance not only of Merlin, but of the angels who guide the planets on their paths, and regulate the lives of their inhabitants. These angels arrive at his house, whose other inhabitants become in turn mercurial, venereal (but decorously so), martial, saturnine, and jovial, but fortunately not lunatic. Merlin and the angels smash up the National Institute and a small university town, Frost and Wither are damned, and Ransom ascends into heaven, bound for Venus, where he is to meet Kings Arthur, Melchizedek, and other select humans who escape death. One *Grammarian's Funeral* less, in fact.

The tale is told with very great skill, and the descriptions of celestial landscapes and of human and nonhuman behaviour are often brilliant. I cannot pay Mr. Lewis a higher compliment than to compare him with Dante and Milton; but to make the balance fair I must also compare him with Rolfe (alias Baron Corvo) and Velenovsky. Dante and Milton knew the science of their time, and Dante was well ahead of most of his contemporaries in holding that the earth was round, and that gravity changed direction at its centre; though Milton hedged as to the Copernican system. Mr. Lewis is often incorrect, as in his account of the gravitational field in the spaceship, of the atmosphere on Mars, the appearance of other planets from it, and so on. His accounts of supernatural intervention would have been more impressive had he known more of nature as it actually exists. Of course, the reason is clear enough. Christian mythology incorporated the cosmological theories current eighteen centuries ago. Dante found it a slight strain to combine this mythology with the facts known in his own day. Milton found it harder. Mr. Lewis finds it impossible.

Mr. Lewis is a teacher of English literature at Oxford.

The philologist Ransom reminds me irresistibly of the idealised Rolfe who becomes Pope as Hadrian VII; though of course it is even more distinguished to escape death by ascending into heaven than to become a pope. Velenovsky (whose name is not so well known) was (or perhaps is) a botanist who discovered a new species of primrose in the Balkans, and called it *Primula deorum,* the primrose of the gods. With such a name one might expect a plant even nobler than the purple giants of the Himalayas and Yunnan. Unfortunately it is a wretched little flower, which will not bear comparison with any of our four British species. In his attempts to defend Christianity, Mr. Lewis has also defended the beliefs in astrology, black magic, Atlantis, and even polytheism; for the planetary angels are called gods, perhaps in deference to Milton. Many sincere Christians will think that he has done no more service to Jesus than Velenovsky to Jupiter.

As a scientist I am particularly interested in his attitude to my profession. There is one decent scientist in the three books, a physicist who is murdered by the devil-worshippers before we have got to know him. The others have an ideology which ranges from a Kiplingesque contempt for "natives" to pure "national socialism," with the devil substituted for the God whose purposes Hitler claimed to carry out. As a matter of fact, very few scientists of any note outside Germany and Italy have become Fascists. In France only one, the engineer Claude, did so, though the Catholic biologist Carrel came back from the U.S.A. to support the Vichy government. A very much larger fraction of the clerical, legal, and literary professions bowed the knee to Baal.

Weston is recognisable as a scientist; Frost and Wither, the devil-worshippers, are not. They talk like some of the less efficient of the Public Relations Officers who defend Big Business, and even Mr. Lewis did not dare to assign them to any particular branch of science. At a guess I should put them as psychologists who had early deserted the scientific aspect of psychology for its mythological developments.

Mr. Lewis's idea is clear enough. The application of science to human affairs can only lead to hell. This world is largely run by the Devil. "The shadow of one dark wing is over all Tellus," and the best we can do is to work out our own salvation in fear and trembling. Revealed religion tells us how to do this. Any human attempts at a planned world are merely playing into the hands of the Devil. Auld Hornie, by the way, to use the pet name which the Scots have given him, perhaps in thanks for his attacks on the Sabbath, has been in charge of our planet since before life originated on it. He even had a swipe at Mars, and removed much of its atmosphere. Some time in the future Jesus and the good angels will take our planet over from him. Meanwhile the Church is a resistance movement, but liberation must await a celestial D-Day. The destruction of Messrs. Frost and Wither was only a commando operation comparable with the bombardment of Sodom and Gomorrah.

In so far as Mr. Lewis succeeds in spreading his views, the results are fairly predictable. He will not have much influence on scientists, if only because he does not know enough science for this purpose. But he will influence public opinion and that of politicians, particularly in Britain. I do not know if he is a best seller in America. He will in no way discourage the more inhuman developments of science, such as the manufacture of atomic bombs. But he will make things more difficult for those who are trying to apply science to human betterment, for example to get some kind of world organisation of food supplies into being, or to arrive at physiological standards for housing. In such cases we scientists are always told that we are treating human beings as animals. Of course we are. My technical assistant keeps a lot of mosquitoes in my laboratory. Their infantile mortality is considerably below that of my own species in most countries, and I hope to get it down below the level of English babies. But meanwhile I should be very happy if all human babies had as good a chance of growing up as my mosquito larvae. Mr. Lewis is presumably more concerned with their baptism, which is alleged to have a large effect on their prospects after death.

More and more, among people who think about such matters, the division is appearing between those who think it is worth while working for a better future (which, since the various members of our species now form, for some purposes, a single community, must be a better future for all mankind) and those who think that the best we can do is to look after our immediate neighbours and our noble selves. Clearly anyone who believes that he or she stands to lose by social changes will be pleased to find arguments to prove that they are impracticable or even devilish. So Mr. Lewis is a most useful prop to the existing social order, the more so as his Martian creatures seem to practise some kind of primitive communism under angelic guidance; so a good Lewisite can get a full measure of self-satisfaction from condemning capitalism as a by-product of the fall of man, while taking no concrete steps to replace it by a better system.

It is interesting to see how Mr. Lewis's ideology has affected his writing. He must obviously be compared with Wells and Stapledon, rather than with the American school of "scientifiction," which is a somewhat lower form of literature than the detective story. The criteria for fictional writing on scientific subjects are similar to those for historical romance. The historical novelist may add to established history. He must not deny it. He may describe the unknown private life of Hal o' the Wynd or Fair Rosamund. He must not contradict what little is known about them without sound reason given. In a scientific romance new processes or substances may be postulated, for example Cavorite, which is opaque to gravitation, or animals which reproduce by clouds of pollen. But apart from special cases our existing knowledge of the properties of matter should be respected. Wells occasionally broke this rule; for example, the giants in *The Food of the Gods* would have broken their legs at every step; but much may be forgiven a pioneer. Stapledon is more scrupulous. Lewis's contempt for science is constantly letting him down. I wish he would learn more, if only because if he did so he would come to respect it. I do not complain of his angels or "eldils." If there are finite superhuman beings they may well be as he describes. I do complain when, in the preface to *The Great Divorce*, he writes: "A wrong sum can be put right: but only by going back till you find the error and working afresh from that point, never by simply going on." I happen to be an addict of the kind of "sum" called iteration. For example, I have recently had to solve the cubic equation

$$7009X^3 - 7470X^2 - 7801X + 516 = 0$$

This equation arises in the theory of mosquito breeding.

Writing it as

$$X = \frac{516}{7801} - X^2 \left[1 - X - \frac{(331 - 792X)}{7801} \right]$$

I put $X = \cdot 06$ on the right-hand side, and get $X = \cdot 0629$ as a better approximation. Then I substitute this value on the right-hand side, and so on, finally getting $X = \cdot 06261$. If I make a small mistake it gets corrected automatically, and may even speed up the approach to the final result. I think the process of solving a moral problem, for example of arriving at mutually satisfactory relations with a colleague, is a good deal more like iteration than the ordinary method of solving such equations.

If Mr. Lewis would learn mathematics and science he might change his views on other matters, for he is intelligent enough to make some very awkward if unconscious admissions. For example, the sinless creatures on Mars had a theology but no religion. They believed in a creator and an after-life, like Benjamin Franklin and other great rationalists; but during a stay of several months among them Mr. Ransom reported no religious ceremonies, or even private prayers. Their conversations with passing angels, or "eldils," whom they occasionally saw and heard, were no more like religious acts than is turning on the radio to listen to Mr. Attlee. This is entirely what one would expect if Mr. Lewis's other premises were true. A person fully adapted to his environment would have no religion. As Marx [1] put it: "This state, this society, produce religion—an inverted consciousness of the world—because it is an inverted world. . . . It is the fantastic realisation of man, because man possesses no true realisation."

Again, it is striking that communism is only once mentioned in the books under review, and though in *The Great Divorce* the narrator finds one Communist in hell, he had left the party and become a conscientious objector in 1941; so perhaps the punishment was deserved, if unduly severe. I take it that Mr. Lewis, who is at least aware of the important difference between right and wrong, though he draws what seems to me to be an incorrect line between them, recognises that Communists also take right and wrong seriously, and is therefore loath to condemn them radically. In consequence the conflict described in *That Hideous Strength*, which is supposed to be important for the future of humanity, lacks reality. And in so far as Mr. Lewis persuades anyone that devil-worship is any more important than other rare perversions, he is merely pandering to moral escapism by diverting his readers from the great moral problems of our day.

I fear that Mr. Lewis is too "bent," to use his own word, to become a communist. Look at his taste in grammar. In the celestial language, of which he gives us some samples, the plurals of the words eldil, pfifltrigg, oyarsa, and hnakra, are eldila, Pfifltriggi, oyéresu, and hnéraki. If that is his ideal of grammar, no wonder his ideals of society are peculiar. Parenthetically, I should have thought the most striking character of a language used by sinless beings who loved their neighbours as themselves would have been the absence of any equivalent of the word "my" and very probably of the word "I," and of other personal pronouns and inflexions.

Nevertheless, if Mr. Lewis investigates the facts honestly, he will probably discover two things. One is that if

Christianity (in the sense of an attempt to follow the precepts attributed to Jesus) has a future, that future, as things are today, is far more likely to be realised within the Orthodox Church than the western Churches. In fact, Marxism may prove to have given Christianity a new lease of life. The second is that scientists are less likely than any other group to sell their souls to the devil. A few of us sell our souls to capitalists and politicians, and Mr. Lewis may have met some such vendors at Oxford. But on the whole we possess moral and intellectual standards, and live up to them as often as other people.

I think we even do so a little more often, because we possess objective standards which others do not. One can find out whether samarium is heavier than lead, whether dogs are more variable in weight than cats, or whether trilobites or dinosaurs lived earliest. There is no way of finding out whether Crashaw was a better poet than Vaughan, or whether Shakespeare wrote the parts for his heroines to suit the leading boy actors of the moment. We also have to risk our lives in the course of our profession rather more often than writers. "The real importance of scientific war," says Mr. Frost, "is that scientists have to be reserved." It is worth remembering that some of us were reserved to unscrew magnetic mines and to test a variety of rather unpleasant chemical substances on our own persons.

But my main quarrel with Mr. Lewis is not for his attack on my profession, but for his attack on my species. I believe that, without any supernatural promptings, men can be extremely good or extremely bad. He must explain human evil by the Devil, and human virtue by God. For him, human freedom is a mere choice between alternatives presented to our souls by supernatural beings. For me it is something creative, in the sense that each generation makes newer and greater possibilities of good and evil. I do not think that Shaw is a greater dramatist than Shakespeare; but some of his characters, for example, Saint Joan, Lavinia, or even Dudgeon, are morally better than any of Shakespeare's characters. Good has grown in three hundred years. So has evil. I do not think that any of the Popes whom Dante saw in hell had done an action as evil as that of Pius XI when he blessed fascism in the encyclical *Quadragesimo Anno.*

Mr. Lewis's characters are confronted with moral choices like slugs in an experimental cage who get a cabbage if they turn right and an electric shock if they turn left. This is no doubt one step nearer to the truth than a completely mechanistic view, but only one step. Two thousand years ago some people had got further. I find Horace's *"justum et tenacem propositi virum,"* who is not deflected by mobs, tyrants, or the great hand of thundering Jove, a vastly more admirable figure than Mr. Lewis's saints who are *"Servile to all the skyey influences"*; though of course Cato's idea of justice was as narrow as ours will, I hope, seem two thousand years hence. But it was men with this Horatian ideal of dignity who made Rome, and men with not very dissimilar ideals who made China, which did not fall as Rome fell. Both the Roman and Chinese ideals were aristocratic. They had to be so in societies where most men and women spent much of their time as mere sources of mechanical power. Today a society is technically possibly where every man and woman can have the leisure and culture needed to take a part in managing it. Democracy is in fact a possibility, but so far it has only worked rather spasmodically. Some of us want to make it a reality. Mr. Lewis regards it as impossible. "There must be rule," says an aged and learned Martian, "yet how can creatures rule themselves? Beasts must be ruled by men, men by angels, and angels by the creator" (I translate several celestial words). As angels do not give most of us very explicit orders, it would seem that we should entrust our destinies to someone like Dr. Frank Buchman or the Pope, who claims to be divinely guided. If Mr. Lewis does not mean us to draw such a conclusion, what does he mean by this passage?

In practice these self-styled mouthpieces of higher powers will presumably transmit orders very similar to Mr. Lewis's broadcast talks on *Christian Behaviour.* They will probably, for example, condemn sodomy absolutely, but they will hedge regarding usury if they even mention it. Mr. Lewis admits that Christian, Jewish, and pagan moralists condemned it, but points out that our society is based on it, and adds: "Now it may not follow that we are absolutely wrong." If it had followed that usury was absolutely wrong, Mr. Lewis's series of radio talks might have been brought to a sudden end like one of Mr. Priestley's. I mention sodomy and usury together because Dante, who expressed the ideals of medieval Christianity, exposed sodomites and usurers to the same rain of flames in hell, with the difference that the sodomites could dodge them, but the usurers (or, as we should say, financiers) could not. If sodomy were an important part of our social system, as it was of some past systems, Mr. Lewis would presumably wonder whether sodomy was absolutely wrong.

The men and women who believe most in human dignity are fighting usury and every other institution which makes man the slave of money. Those who share Mr. Lewis's view are compromising with these evils in one way or another, even if they do not always attack democracy as openly as does Mr. Lewis. Any Marxist can see why this must be so; and Christian readers of Mr. Lewis's books might well remember St. James's statement: "Whosoever therefore will be a friend of the world is the enemy of God." His books certainly have very large sales, and may have a very large influence. It is only for this reason that they are worth attacking. They can of course be attacked on many other grounds than those which I have given. But I would state my case briefly as follows. I agree with Mr. Lewis that man is in a sense a fallen being. *The Origin of the Family* seems to me to provide better evidence for this belief than the Book of Genesis. But I disagree with him in that I also believe that man can rise again by his own efforts. Those who hold the contrary view inevitably regard the reform of society as a dangerous dream, and natural science as unworthy of serious study. And they consequently end up by making friends with the mammon of unrighteousness. But this friendship, so far from qualifying them for an eternal habitation, may not even secure them a competence in this present world. For Mammon has been cleared off a sixth of our planet's surface, and his realm is contracting in Europe today. It was men, not angels, who cast him out.

Some Psychological Aspects of Lewis's Trilogy

ROBERT PLANK

C. S. Lewis was, for which we should be thankful, para-doxical: a science fiction writer who did not write real science fiction; a Christian who ranged far away from the inherited world of Christianity; a novelist whose works were not, in any ordinary sense, novels.

His famed trilogy consists of three of them, *Out of the Silent Plant, Perelandra,* and *That Hideous Strength,*[1] though it has been argued that there really is no trilogy—that only the first two novels are closely related to each other. I shall stay out of this controversy, and this may be a good place to list other things that I shall not attempt: I shall stay away, as far as possible, from literary criticism. Lewis distinguished "the genuinely critical question, 'why and how should we read this?'" from the "purely histori-cal question, 'why did he write it?'"[2] I address myself to this second question (to which may be added, why does it appeal to readers?). I shall not try either to fix Lewis's place in literary history, or to discuss his religious, philo-sophical, or political ideas.

This paper will not attempt more than what its title implies, with emphasis on the "some." Its purpose is to stimulate thought on the questions the three books raise, rather than to solve them. It may not be possible to give unambiguous answers anyway. Goethe said that his works were all "fragments of a great confession," and this may well apply to any great imaginative writer.

As far as he can and will, the writer shows in his works how he has come to terms with the great issues that are also the objects of psychological study: birth and death;

the role of man—and his own role in particular—in the world; love and hate (or sex and aggression). These are the "fragments." Their challenge is threefold: to consider each for what it reveals; to trace its special characteristics to the author's life history; to look beyond them for a unifying principle, for the features that emanate from the core of the personality to give the writer his uniqueness.

The task of psychological analysis is to put the confession together from the fragments. In endeavoring to do so, I shall lean on what Lewis says in the trilogy, using extraneous material only occasionally, to make explicit what in the three novels, since they are fiction, can only be implicit.

The author's emotional involvement often comes out clearest in the way he shapes the figure of the hero; this is true of Lewis. The most obvious connecting link between his three books is that they each tell of a great adventure that befalls the same person, Dr. Elwin Ransom. There are few other links: a unity of purpose, of message, of the author's philosophy, religion, ethos, call it what you will —but this would be true of all his works; and a secondary villain, Devine, but his role in the third book (as Lord Feverstone) is rather unimportant (the primary villain, Professor Weston, has been killed in the second book).

That the hero is thus virtually the only link enhances his importance. Now normally in such a case the author would elaborate the portrait; he would add. Lewis does rather the opposite. He subtracts. As the trilogy progresses, Ransom's features are shed. He becomes less individual and more an allegory. Growing more exalted, he becomes less human.

At the beginning he is "tall, but a little round-shouldered, about thirty-five to forty years of age, and dressed with that peculiar kind of shabbiness which marks a member of the intelligentsia on a holiday. He might easily have been mistaken for a doctor or a schoolmaster at first sight" (O, 3).

Toward the end Jane Studdock is introduced to him, "and instantly her world was unmade. On a sofa before

her . . . lay what appeared to be a boy, twenty years old.
. . . All the light in the room seemed to run toward the
gold hair and the gold beard of the . . . man. Of course
he was not a boy. . . . It came over her that this face was
of no age at all" (*T*, 84). Of course, he has been on Mars
and Venus in between. He has saved one world and is
about to save one more.

He has retained little of his old self except his names —
but what names! Lewis explains the Christian name easily
enough, though he gives to the commonplace fact (most
of our names have such origins) a peculiar twist: "His
very name in his own language is Elwin, the friend of the
Eldila" (*P*, 208). The explanation of *Ransom* is more
arresting: it is "the name of a payment that delivers" (*P*,
154). At the very climax of the story, as the crucial appeal
that changes everything, the Voice — and there is no mis-
taking whose voice it is — says: "My name also is Ransom"
ibid.).

There is also a third name, and a title. We had learned
in *Out of the Silent Planet*, chapter two, that Ransom
had a married sister in India. As we reach *That Hideous
Strength*, chapter five, she has died and bequeathed him
her money and her name — Fisher-King.

Sister in India indeed! The name evokes the man who
was to become a fisher of men and a spiritual ruler, but
more significantly, "fisher-king" is specifically the title of
the master of the knights of the Holy Grail in the medieval legend. This ruler (since Wagner's *Parsifal* better
known as Amfortas) suffers from an unhealing wound, as
Ransom does. The fertility of the land depends on the life
and health of the Fisher-King.[3] This is the motive to
which T. S. Eliot alludes at the end of *The Waste Land*.[4]

In addition to "Fisher-King," Ransom has acquired an
even more venerable title: the ancient British designation
of supreme leadership. He has become the Pendragon,
before whom the mightiest of the magicians goes down on
his knee.

These are but terrestrial honors, and those awarded in
the heavens are even higher. The unfallen Adam of an-

other world proclaims upon coming into his kingdom: ". . . this is the first word I speak as Tor-Oyarsa-Perelendri: that in our world, as long as it is a world, neither shall morning come nor night but that we and all our children shall speak to Maleldil of Ransom . . . and praise him to one another . . . in another fashion we call you Lord and Father" (*P*, 222). And at the end of the trilogy we are told that Ransom shall not die: the Lord will keep him in the body to the end, a distinction that had been granted to only six or seven men since the creation of the world.

Let us not forget how extraordinary this is! We very rarely find heroes of this sort outside of the most "low-brow" fiction. Short of making the protagonist a god — no Greek would have had any difficulty here, but to Lewis, a Christian, this was forbidden — it is hard to see how the apotheosis of the hero could go any higher.

To soar to such superhuman stature makes for loneliness. It would be unnatural for the Ransom of the three books to have any true companion on his rise. However, Lewis does not indicate that his hero had any intimate relationships before he was called to high adventure either. That sister in India is his only relative. Of his friends we know little, but chiefly because there is little to know: if he disappears on a walking-tour, he will not be missed for months (*O*, 13–15).

What is more, a peculiar isolation marks the other characters of the trilogy also. Some are only seen in what might be called a professional context, so that the question of their families is left open. Many, however, are shown more completely. Several are married. None of them (apart from quite peripheral figures) have children, and none seem to have living parents.

We must not overlook, of course, that Lewis introduces characters because of the role assigned to them in the cosmic battle between God and the Devil rather than because of their mundane fate. It can not astonish us, therefore, that sex and sexual love are not given emphasis. This does not bespeak prudery on the part of the author; he seems to have been rather free of that blemish. The trilogy simply deals with something else, and to look for love stories in it would be as fatuous as to blame the author of *Othello* and *Romeo and Juliet* for not having put much of a "love interest" into *Macbeth* and *King Lear*.

It thus comes as a shock to the reader to find himself faced with a pronunciamento on sex when he least expects it. The forces of evil, in the guise of the National Institute of Co-ordinated Experiments (the initials, ironically, spell NICE) have almost conquered. The task is laid on Ransom to prevent, in the nick of time, their final triumph. To take part in the ultimate struggle, Merlin is awakened from fifteen hundred years of sleep. As he faces Ransom, he must decide which side he will be on, and Ransom must convince him that he is the Pendragon. About the last thing one would expect them to discuss in this fateful interview, with England in chaos about them and the torture chambers of NICE filling up with victims, is the sexual behavior of man in the Moon. And yet, this is just what they do.

> The Stranger mused for a few seconds; then, speaking in a slightly sing-song voice, he asked the following question:
> "Who is Sulva? What road does she walk? Why is the womb barren on one side? Where are the cold marriages?"
> Ransom replied, "Sulva is she whom mortals call the Moon. She walks in the lowest sphere. Half of her orb is turned towards us and shares our curse. On this side the womb is barren and the marriages cold. There dwell an accursed people, full of pride and lust. There when a man takes a maiden in marriage, they do not lie together, but each lies with a cunningly fashioned image of the other, made to move and to be warm by devilish arts, for real flesh will not please them, they are so dainty (*delicati*) in their dreams of lust. Their real children they fabricate by vile arts in a secret place." (*T*, 166)

It is perhaps needless to say that there is no group of people on Earth (or, for that matter, on either side of the Moon) known to have engaged in practices even remotely comparable to this. What makes the idea still more arresting is that it is offered gratuitously. The tale does not require it in the least—Merlin could just as easily ask about many other things, as he does in his later questions. What is the meaning of this extraordinary fantasy?

A clue is perhaps concealed in the last sentence, for it contains a peculiar echo: "Their real children they fabricate by vile arts in a secret place" sounds almost like a parody (in the sense in which all the Devil does is a parody of what God does) of "My substance was not hid from thee, when I was made in secret, and curiously wrought in the lowest parts of the Earth." This is Verse 15 of Psalm 139. Verse 16 begins, "Thine eyes did see my substance, yet being unperfect. . . ." The Hebrew word for that substance is *golem.* The Bible does not use the word anywhere else. Verse 16 has been the root from which a vigorous growth of legends sprouted, the legends of the golem, a man-made manlike being.

The motive has undergone many changes from the time it is first known to have been recorded in the twelfth century to its presentation in stories, films, and opera in the twentieth, but there is only one instance in which it was given the meaning it has for Lewis's Moon-people, namely in the novel *Isabella in Aegypten* by Achim von Arnim, where the paramour of the Archduke Charles, later Emperor Charles V, is spirited away and replaced by a golem functioning as her double (the myth of Helen in Egypt has another character; her double was made by a god, not by men).

Lewis of course knew Psalm 139. He discussed the golem passage (vss. 13–16) in his *Reflections on the Psalms,* though in a different context (Ikhnaton's *Hymn to the Sun*). That he knew a virtually forgotten German novel of one hundred and fifty years ago is improbable. It seems more likely that the two authors arrived independently at the same fantasy: that the Biblical material (in Arnim's case, by way of Grimm's brief paper on the golem) suggested to them, through the inner logic of the unconscious processes it set in motion, the same idea: the substitution of a man-made counterfeit for the living body of the beloved—which Arnim treats as a great joke, Lewis as a great sin.

Both are the same: reification, a variant of the now so fashionable alienation. That this perversion of the organic sex act into an artificial play with an image is Lewis's major pronouncement on sex in the trilogy, accords well with the one consistent quality of his characters: the impoverished state of their relations with other human beings.

Nowhere else in literature is a golem used as a sexual object. The double of Angela in Charles Williams' *Descent into Hell* is similar to a golem, but is really a figment of a different nature. She is not man-made, but a work of the Devil (p. 138), a "phantom" (p. 145), a "secret creature of substantial illusion" (p. 110), a "magical creature drawn from his [Lawrence Wentworth's] own recesses" (p. 96).[5] While within the fictitious world of the marvellous tale the golem possesses as much reality as a living being, this "phantom" does not (the operational test is that she cannot be perceived by anybody but the man from whose "recesses" she has sprung; Arnim's golem, and presumably Lewis's cunningly fashioned images are perceived by everybody alike).

Translated from Williams' symbolic magical idiom into plainer behavioral language, the pseudo-Angela clearly spells masturbation. The perversion described in Arnim's and Lewis's works is different. It comes closer to Fetishism —in fact, it is one step farther removed from "normal" sexual feeling than the sort of Fetishism which the text-books of psychiatry describe.

Keeping this in mind, we must also note that although Lewis presents his ideas about the sexual practices on the Moon explosively where the course of his novel by no means calls for it, he also makes an effort to connect them with customs not unknown on Earth; but he does so ex post facto, as it were: as Merlin, after his fateful interview with Ransom, sees Jane Studdock, he—being a magician —immediately sees through her and diagnoses her and her husband's case as analogous to that of the "accursed people" on the Moon: "Of their own will they are barren: I did not know till now that the usages of Sulva were so common among you" (*T,* 170). Unimpressed by Ransom's intercession ("She is but lately married—the child may yet be born"), he has his own solution, one that has the advantage of directness: "It would be great charity if you gave order that her head be cut from her shoulders; for it is a weariness to look at her" (*ibid.*).

What is so strange about this is not so much Merlin's punitive approach to the problem, as his misapprehension of it, for obviously, what the Studdocks have practiced is birth control: they want to delay having children until they are more settled. Mark has his full share of faults, but to be dainty (*delicatus*) in his dreams of lust is scarcely one of them. Does he even *have* dreams of lust? "Only one thing ever seemed able to keep him awake after he had gone to bed, and even that did not keep him awake for long" (*T,* 7).

There is, of course, a Christian tradition of condemning birth control, and one psychoanalytic paper [6] has interpreted such practices as aggression against the couple's fathers, but none of this warrants identification of the birth control practices by the Studdocks with the golemistic practices on the Moon. One cannot help feeling that Lewis included the Merlin-Jane episode to provide a belated rationale for his golem fantasy; and that it is this fantasy that really matters to him.

Having thus seen libido withdrawn from interpersonal relations and channelled into the exaltation of the hero, we are now ready to tackle a puzzle that would have baffled us without this preparation. The trilogy is usually classified as science fiction, yet not on any grounds that would stand up to scrutiny. There are many definitions of science fiction, but all agree that this genre is characterized by the prominence of science in its content, by extrapolating from scientific achievements of the past and present, by dealing with things that might be though they have not been. Little of that can be found in the trilogy (except in its third book). Why, then, "science fiction"?

That practitioners of the art should have claimed Lewis as their own can perhaps be explained by their need for a "front man": given the reputation of science fiction as it was, they may well have felt the need to enhance their respectability. But why should Lewis himself,[7] and the scholars who have considered his work, indulge in the same misclassification?

The answer suggests itself that this happened because Lewis plotted *Out of the Silent Planet* and *Perelandra* around the motive of space travel. But space travel is not the same as science fiction. There is much science fiction that has nothing to do with space travel (works like *Brave New World*, or the great bulk of robot stories), and there are space travel stories that are not, by any rational definition, science fiction. Lewis's stories are of just that type: the scientific problems of space travel are brushed aside with a few sentences that give merely an outward semblance of dealing with them, the conditions on the planets visited are described with utter disregard of actual possibilities; for example, the atmosphere on Mars and Venus is supposed to be like that on Earth. Space travel is not what Lewis talks about; it is merely a device to set the stage for what he really has to say.

The identification of the trilogy with science fiction can be justified, however, by a deeper psychological affinity. Though this is not part of any accepted definition, much of that genre is characterized by the same emotional climate that pervades the trilogy: immense aggrandizement of the hero, far beyond anything that would be permissible in realistic fiction; emotional isolation of the characters; a cold attitude toward sex, sometimes embellished with experimentation along lines of other gratification than by so-called normal intercourse; and the replacement of the organic processes of earthly life by the manipulation of artefacts.

There are two other areas in which Lewis's work is akin to much of science fiction. These affinities, though, are not limited to Lewis and science fiction, but are common to the imaginative literature of our time. One is the gusto for violence.

The conflict that forms the theme of *Perelandra* is driven to the point where it is decided by hand-to-hand combat, "naked chest to naked chest" (p. 153). Little detail is spared: ". . . the long metallic nails . . . ripping off narrow strips of flesh, pulling out tendons. . . . He started bending the enemy's left arm back by main force with some idea of breaking it. . . . He felt its ribs break, he heard its jaw-bone crack" (pp. 149, 161, 163).

The fight between good and evil is actually an abstract process. True, to become a narrative it has to be incarnated—but in so much torn flesh? One would think it could be done, without blunting the point of the story, on some level closer to the intrapsychic struggle it really is.

The conflict that *That Hideous Strength* is about is solved by a peerless massacre. It is true here, too, that the logic of the story requires the annihilation of the forces of evil; but hardly of the persons that embody them. Would not Christian virtue shine brighter if the evil scheme were frustrated but the evil-doers were redeemed? True, it is not easy to imagine Miss Hardcastle rehabilitated socially and morally, let alone spiritually, but Lewis has not been an author to shrink from such a tour de force. Here, however, he piles body on body, bloody deed on bloody deed, climaxing it with the apocalyptic scene of the beasts invading the banquet. There is a partial parallel to this in Flaubert's great *St. Julien l'Hôpitalier*. Both massacres epitomize the rebellion of animal nature against the sinful man who violates its order; but Flaubert's animals offer themselves to be massacred, and the sinner is cursed and must finally atone; Lewis's animals massacre the sinful humans. Perhaps this is how the spirits of the nineteenth and the twentieth century differ. It is also hard not to get the impression of Lewis endlessly gloating over all the spilled blood.

The other area where Lewis is truly modern (in the sense in which science fiction is modern) concerns a mood that from its most eminent representative may be called Kafkaesque. Fictional characters conceived in this mood are not tragic, they do not determine their fate. Their actions are the dance of marionettes moved by forces they cannot understand, much less control. The sociological imagination sees herein the reflection of the totally organized mass society that we were already asymptotically approaching in Kafka's time. Lewis is hardly concerned with this. The mood that pervades the trilogy differs in the balance of forces: though sinister powers are not absent, they are, in contrast to Kafka, subordinate. But the similarity is also marked. Lewis's world has no room for chance, everything has meaning. Every action has long been planned, though not by the man who acts.

This view of man's destiny reflects Lewis's belief in God, but also modifies it. The modification mirrors his image of his father who also had planned everything and whom he could neither understand nor control, as his autobiography, *Surprised by Joy*, supplemented by other sources, makes clear. The struggling advance from his view of his father to the view of his God left its trace in the progression of the novels. At the beginning of each, the sinister powers set the mood: in *Out of the Silent Planet*, we have Ransom on his walking-tour, having to look for a place to stay and stumbling into the lair of the villains who accept him as victim in lieu of a feeble-minded boy—stumbling, that is (but of course, only seemingly stumbling) into his, and a world's, destiny. In *Perelandra*, Lewis, walking to Ransom's cottage, is constantly repelled by vague anxieties that are soon unmasked as the influence of inimical powers. In *That Hideous Strength*, there is Jane's clairvoyant and equally discomforting dream. These are the starts, all set in dismal nights. Each novel describes a triumphant sunrise, as it were, and the end of each is glory.

In discussing Lewis's hero, the role of emotional isolation, sex, and violence in the trilogy, and Lewis's view of the powers that shape man's fate, I have tried to sketch how the "fragments" may be put together into the "confession." This cannot yield more than the author can and will confess. There are many parts to this structure, all on the surface. Turning now to the second task of psychological analysis, the tracing of the work to the writer's life history, I shall limit myself to a single example.

Lewis puts his imagined Mars and Venus before us so vividly, in such corporeal reality, that we not only believe (while we read) such improbable worlds to exist, but also that we get immersed in them to the extent of believing that we see, feel, smell them. All writers of heterotopias (science fiction, utopias, and related types of tales) have attempted this, but few have so gloriously succeeded. It is a very special talent Lewis exerted here, and in his case it is easy to see how he developed it, for he explained it in his autobiography. He had created a set of fantasies about an "Animal-Land" and began to write stories about it before he was ten ("I wrote about chivalrous mice and rabbits who rode out in complete mail to kill not giants but cats. . ."). Before he was fifteen, Animal-Land and his brother's "India" had merged "into the single state of Boxen," a country with two kings, a legislative assembly, a prime minister; at one time that office was held by a frog.

These buds were to blossom out into Malacandra and Perelandra; but where were the roots? As always in historical research, every cause that is found is in itself an effect that asks for a more remote cause. W. H. Lewis, the author's brother, traces their joint early imaginings to the combined effect of the climate of their native Northern Ireland and of the child-rearing practices of the time.[8] These would be objective facts, but the words in which he speaks of them ("this recurring imprisonment . . . that childhood staring out to unattainable hills") make it clear how they were reflected in feelings. C. S. Lewis's mother died in his tenth year. His relationship to his father was never easy or cordial. To trace anything farther back would be a task almost impossible to discharge. Ignorance would hamper the pursuit, and where it were removed discretion might forbid it. I can leave it with ease of mind, having said that I aim at stimulating thought rather than at answering questions, and so I am turning to the third task of psychological analysis.

The question here is, can we find a peculiar emotional set at the core of the author's personality to explain the unique flavor of his work? Or, if we want to put it negatively, is there any quality that would have given his personality a peculiar twist if his talent had not allowed him to sublimate it into his unique work? If I dare to take such a course, it might reinforce a feeling that the reader may have developed, with growing discomfort—that I have come to bury Lewis, not to praise him; but here I can also call on a witness to testify that this endeavor is not illicit: Lewis's friend, Owen Barfield, says in his introduction to *Light on C. S. Lewis* that the author as a young man "had been quite aware of the technique of diagnosing the psyche in terms of its latent perversion—and quite capable of applying this technique to himself, and incidentally to me." Though it may not be entirely clear what technique is meant, it is not method as such that matters, and we consider ourselves authorized to proceed.

An outstanding feature of *Perelandra*—indeed, the outstanding charm of the book—is the description of the new, unearthly perceptions that are constantly vouchsafed to Ransom. Since it is their totality that creates the enchanting mood, scraps will only convey a faint echo, but we must have a few examples:

> the darkness was warm. Sweet new scents came stealing out of it. The world had no size now. Its boundaries were the length and breadth of his own body and the little patch of soft fragrance which made his hammock, swaying ever more and more gently (p. 40).
>
> Over his head there hung from a hairy tube-like branch a great spherical object, almost transparent, and shining. . . . He put out his hand to touch it. Immediately his head, face, and shoulders were drenched with what seemed (in that warm world) an ice-cold shower bath, and his nostrils filled with a sharp, shrill, exquisite scent that somehow brought to his mind the verse in Pope, "die of a rose in aromatic pain" (p. 43).
>
> Darting pillars filled with eyes, lightning pulsations of flame, talons and beaks and billowy masses of what suggested snow, volleyed through cubes and heptagons into an infinite black void. . . . Far off between the peaks on the other side of the little valley there came rolling wheels. . . . And suddenly two human figures stood before him on the opposite side of the lake (p. 211).

Has anything like this been seen, felt, smelled on
Earth? It has:

> The present author, at the time of his first LSD-inges-
> tion . . . floated graciously through lovely caverns of spar-
> kling ice and splendid, gold-encrusted Gothic cathedrals,
> and watched in awe as jeweled patterns formed and re-
> formed in an endless variety of living mandalar shapes.[9]
>
> Far above me, many-hued, its giant wings fluttering, the
> great jeweled moth descends.[10] . . . "all at once" colors are
> bright and glowing, the outlines of objects are defined as
> they never have been before, spatial relationships are dras-
> tically altered, several or all of the senses are enormously
> heightened—"all at once" the world has shed its older,
> everyday façade and stands revealed as a wonderland.[11]
>
> Half an hour after swallowing the drug I became aware
> of a slow dance of golden lights. A little later there were
> sumptuous red surfaces swelling and expanding from
> bright nodes of energy that vibrated with a continuously
> changing, patterned life.[12]

The parallel is close. That is, the contents of the experience are similar—not at all the way it was produced.
Lewis achieved his by a pure effort of the imagination, the
others describe experiences they obtained by ingesting
"consciousness-expanding" drugs. The term would not be
alien to Lewis. In a talk on science fiction delivered in
1955 he said, "Good stories of this sort"—that is, stories
where "the marvellous is in the grain of the whole work"
—"are actual additions to life: they give, like certain rare
dreams, sensations we never had before, and enlarge our
conception of the range of possible experience."

A man's mind, however much expanded, is an organic
whole, and if we try to reconstruct his confession from the
fragments, especially if we do so with the benefit of
insights arrived at by psychoanalysis, we need to see it as a
whole. We see the writer's inner conflicts reflected—but
also purified by having been filtered through the creative
process—in his work. We see the bonds of ordinary relationships loosened, sex mechanized and shorn of its
attractions, the energies thus freed poured into the apoth-

eosis of the hero and into the joy of imaginary worlds closer to the heart's desire, we see banal striving replaced by the enlargement of the range of sensual experience. To understand the emotional world of the creator of such works should help to understand the works more deeply and to enjoy them more.

It is in this sense that I think the comparison of *Perelandra* and psychedelics yields a fresh insight into Lewis's personality. It reveals a motive force that gives his work its unique savor as the same that drives others to seek "mind-expanding" drugs: the desire for sensual experiences beyond those that come to man in the normal course of his life. His talent enabled him to reach this goal unaided where those without the talent need the drugs—or, to put it in a consciously oversimplified form, had it not been for that Animal-Land and Boxen, he might have become a devotee of LSD.

Such a view does not detract from appreciation of Lewis's nobility, for this is not an ignoble goal. It rather adds a trait of nobility to the picture of those who, lacking Lewis's talent, need the drugs for similar achievement (and their banishment is uncomfortably reminiscent of the tyranny of a research bureaucracy in *That Hideous Strength*). Perhaps we have come to praise Lewis, not to bury him, after all.

Out of the Silent Planet as Cosmic Voyage

MARK R. HILLEGAS

Most recent exegesis of C. S. Lewis's *Out of the Silent Planet*, *Perelandra*, and *That Hideous Strength* has been devoted to illuminating Lewis's use of myth in the "cosmic trilogy." [1] Underlying the trilogy—a *Paradise Lost* written for our unsuspecting, skeptical twentieth century—is, of course, the "silent planet" myth. Since the war in heaven, Earth (called Thulcandra in Old Solar) has been quarantined from the rest of the universe to prevent the spread of its spiritual infection. In *Out of the Silent Planet* the barrier is broken when Ransom, the Cambridge philogist, is kidnapped and taken to Malacandra or Mars (an unfallen world) by two men, Weston and Devine, who mistakenly believe a human sacrifice is necessary to further their purposes on that world. A new chapter in the history of the universe is thus begun, and in *Perelandra* Ransom journeys to Venus, a new world, where he plays a major part in averting a second Fall. In *That Hideous Strength* the forces of Earth's Bent One (Satan) are prevented from turning our world into a godless scientific state by a small band gathered around the now Christ-like Ransom, who is aided by the Arthurian Merlin and the forces of Deep Heaven, now able at last to enter the circle of the moon and reach the Earth. Lewis's three books appeal both to literary people who value myth for itself and to Christians who treasure the trilogy's presentation of Christian theology in a new idiom.

Indeed, readers and critics are so taken with Lewis's use of myth that they tend to underrate the first volume, *Out of the Silent Planet.* If they like Lewis, they, of course, like all three parts of the trilogy, but *Out of the Silent Planet* stands lower in their estimation than the second and third books, especially the third. I would like to argue here that *Out of the Silent Planet,* seen for what it really is and not just as a mythic presentation of Christian doctrine, is a considerably better work than it is at the moment thought to be.

Out of the Silent Planet (1938) differs greatly from the two later volumes. One very good reason for this is that it was written before Lewis came to know Charles Williams very well. *That Hideous Strength* (1945) shows the strong influence of Williams' "theological thrillers"; and even *Perelandra* (1943) shows Lewis moving in the direction of Williams. Although Lewis managed to fit all three books together and to give them the unity of their underlying myth, *Out of the Silent Planet* is a very different sort of book from either *Perelandra* or *That Hideous Strength.*

What has been forgotten in most recent discussions is that *Out of the Silent Planet* is a splendid representative of a very old genre, the "cosmic voyage." It is this before it is anything else, and really to judge it properly one must know how it is a "cosmic voyage." Of all the numerous examples of the genre discussed in Marjorie Nicolson's *Voyages to the Moon,* only two (excluding satiric cosmic voyages, such as Voltaire's *Micromegas*) are significant as literature. One is H. G. Wells's *The First Men in the Moon* (1901), and the other is *Out of the Silent Planet.* Ironically, these two stand at the end of the tradition, the last of their kind. (I should note here that, although *Perelandra* is set on Venus, it is more theological fantasy than cosmic voyage; Ransom, for example, is transported to the new world by supernatural means.)

The cosmic voyage had its origin in the seventeenth century when, under the impact of the new astronomy, particularly through the invention of the telescope and the discovery of a world in the moon, men began to consider the problems of travel to another world. The cosmic voyages which resulted—such as Kepler's *Som-*

nium (1634), Godwin's *Man in the Moone* (1638), and Cyrano de Bergerac's *Voyages to the Sun and Moon* (1650)—established the form of the genre until as late as the fourth decade of the twentieth century and *Out of the Silent Planet.*

The cosmic voyage fits neatly into Wellek and Warren's formula for defining genre by outer and inner form. Outer form is usually prose fiction. Inner form includes a fixed subject matter—an imaginary journey to another world in space—and certain stereotyped conventions, such as the *bouleversement* and weightlessness; the exhilarating sensations of space travel (usually a feeling of disembodiment); the Earth seen as a great globe leisurely turning before the voyager; and, of course, the landing on a strange new world. Inner form also includes a fixed *Kunstwollen:* the aesthetic intent to convey the "abiding strangeness" of the journey through space and the landing on another world. Although this has been the aesthetic intent of the cosmic voyage for three centuries, a change of tone took place in the cosmic voyage in the nineteenth century.

Essentially the shift in tone was the result of a greater effort at realism. In their treatment of the journey itself, seventeenth and eighteenth-century writers manifested some scientific imagination, even though they had no clear conception of the nature of space as a cold, airless void and sent their travelers to the moon, planets, and sun in vehicles which seem utterly fantastic to the sophisticated twentieth century. But in their description of the worlds on which their travelers landed, early writers, with the exception of Kepler, turned to previous literature, borrowing from the utopian tradition and from such familiar sources of fantasy as the "extraordinary voyages" of Rabelais' *Pantagruel,* Astolfo's visit to the moon in Ariosto's *Orlando Furioso,* or Lucian's *True History.*

In the nineteenth century a quite different spirit came to dominate the cosmic voyage as the result of accelerating advances in science and technology, advances which brought new knowledge of the principles of flight, the

nature of space, and the limits of the atmosphere as well
as the discoveries based upon the descriptive astronomy
which Sir William Herschel inaugurated. Instead of the
unrestrained imaginativeness—the science in the journey
notwithstanding—which had previously characterized the
cosmic voyage, the genre became more concerned with
achieving the appearance of realism as writers lavished
greater and greater attention on the technical details of
the spaceship, the voyage through the void of space, and
the new world. The first appearance of this new realism
was probably George Tucker's A Voyage to the Moon
(1827), but a more significant manifestation was Poe's
"The Unparalleled Adventures of One Hans Pfaal"
(1835), a narrative of a trip to the moon in a balloon of
amazing buoyancy. Unfortunately, "Hans Pfaal" is one of
Poe's least successful stories, failing precisely because Poe
attempted to yoke old fantasy, in the form of an envelop-
ing plot, with a severely realistic account of the voyage
itself (including a description of a sealed car with appara-
tus for condensing air and even an encounter with a
meteor, the extraterrestrial origins of which had only recently been established). Various extremely minor cosmic
voyages followed Poe's, each attempting to blend in one
way or another old fantasy and new realism, until the new
spirit triumphed in Verne's From the Earth to the Moon
and Round the Moon (1865 and 1870), the first major
cosmic voyage completely to discard the old fantasy. This
story, in which the ballistics experts of the Baltimore Gun
Club shoot a projectile with three passengers around the
moon and back to earth, bristles with mathematical calcu-
lations and facts about the moon and space; it firmly
established the new realistic tone and high seriousness
about space travel of the modern cosmic voyage.

There is, of course, an enormous difference between
Verne's moon saga on the one hand and Wells's The First
Men in the Moon and C. S. Lewis's Out of the Silent
Planet on the other. It is not just that the stories by Wells
and Lewis are infinitely better written; it is also that they
make better imaginative use of their materials, avoiding

Verne's sin of overloading his stories with facts and details. At the same time, however, it must be emphasized that Wells and Lewis, like Verne, wrote cosmic voyages which were modern in terms of the knowledge of their time: a journey through space and a strange other world, plausible in terms of what physics, astronomy, biology, and other sciences revealed as to the conditions of space and the possibility of interplanetary travel, the physical nature of other planets, and the requirements for the origin and evolution of life.

It is important here to emphasize the contrast between recent space fiction and *The First Men in the Moon* or *Out of the Silent Planet*. Much has been lost: for one thing, the awesome and heroic imaginative event of the journey through star-dusted space. Usually the space novel or story, unless specifically concerned with some aspect of the journey—for example, human reaction to the several generations of time required to reach the stars—has been able to presuppose the voyage and all its conventions: the tale usually begins with the adventurer already in space or on another world, and, if the voyage must be described, it is handled in a few paragraphs or sentences, sometimes as flatly as in this opening sentence from Robert Heinlein's "The Black Pits of Luna": "The morning after we got to the Moon, we went over to Rutherford." The imaginative loss has been well described by Robert Plank.

> Imagine, if you can, Odysseus without the eternally foaming waves; Joseph Conrad's captains and mates without ever feeling a storm against their bodies; Hemingway's Old Man never going out to fish; imagine the whole world's lore and literature of the sea reduced to a description of ships at anchor and sailors in port.[2]

Another loss is the alienness, the unknown strangeness of the other worlds themselves. This has to do with our acclimation to the extraterrestrial, a process accelerated since Russia and the United States began sending men into orbit and which Lewis himself predicted in 1947 in his essay, "On Stories."

If some fatal progress of applied science ever enables us in fact to reach the Moon, that real journey will not at all satisfy the impulse which we now seek to gratify by writing such stories. The real Moon, if you could reach it and survive, would in a deep and deadly sense be just like anywhere else.[3]

Almost all the stock conventions of the cosmic voyage are incorporated in Lewis's narrative of the journey to Mars—such as, for example, the tinkling missiles, which are meteorites, and the Earth as a great globe hanging in space. While Lewis, as Miss Nicolson suggests, was probably acquainted with the whole tradition of the cosmic voyage, the most immediate ancestor of *Out of the Silent Planet*, and particularly its journey through space, was *The First Men in the Moon*—which is hardly surprising, in view of how highly Lewis admired *The First Men in the Moon*. He spoke often of the story, admitting that he had grown up on it (and other of Wells's scientific romances) and praising it as the "best of the sort I have read." [4] His prefatory note to the book is devoted to acknowledging his debt to Wells:

Certain slighting references to earlier stories of this type which will be found in the following pages have been put there for purely dramatic purposes. The author would be sorry if any reader supposed he was too stupid to have enjoyed Mr. H. G. Wells' fantasies or too ungrateful to acknowledge his debt to them.[5]

Out of the Silent Planet follows the same general strategy used in *The First Men in the Moon* to "domesticate the incredible." Where Wells starts with the everyday and ordinary details of Kent and makes "solid and credible" the characters of Bedford and Cavor before introducing the remarkable antigravity substance Cavorite and the miraculous journey to the Moon, Lewis begins with Ransom, the Cambridge philogist, on a walking-tour somewhere in the Midlands. The opening paragraph, rich in circumstantial details, immediately convinces us of the integrity of the storyteller and the truth of the story.

The last drops of the thundershower had hardly ceased falling when the Pedestrian stuffed his map into his pocket, settled his pack more comfortably on his tired shoulders, and stepped out from the shelter of a large chestnut-tree into the middle of the road. A violent yellow sunset was pouring through a rift in the clouds to westward, but straight ahead over the hills the sky was the colour of dark slate. Every tree and blade of grass was dripping, and the road shone like a river. The Pedestrian wasted no time on the landscape but set out at once with the determined stride of a good walker who has lately realized that he will have to walk farther than he intended. (OSP, 1)

The Pedestrian becomes Ransom, who by a series of incidents in themselves earthly and credible, though increasingly sinister, wakes up a captive in Weston and Devine's spaceship. Though he is startled, we are not, for the foreshadowing of this event has been carefully prepared.

The ship is Cavor and Bedford's sphere, including even the steel blinds (though they serve a different purpose). The purposively vague explanation of the principle of propulsion echoes Bedford's attempt at a nontechnical explanation of Cavor's invention of a substance "opaque" to gravity.

As to how we do it—I suppose you mean how the spaceship works—there's no good your asking that. Unless you were one of the four or five real physicists now living you couldn't understand. . . . If it makes you happy to repeat words that don't mean anything—which is, in fact, what unscientific people want when they ask for an explanation —you may say we work by exploiting the less observed properties of solar radiation. (OSP, 22)

In its poetry, the journey is very much like Cavor and Bedford's trip through star-dusted space.

There was endless night on one side of the ship and an endless day on the other: each was marvellous and he moved from the one to the other at his will, delighted. In the nights, which he could create by turning the handle of a door, he lay for hours in contemplation of the skylight. The Earth's disk was nowhere to be seen; the stars, thick as daisies on an uncut lawn, reigned perpetually with no cloud, no moon, no sunrise to dispute their sway. There were planets of unbelievable majesty, and constellations undreamed of: there were celestial sapphires, rubies, emeralds and pin-pricks of burning gold; far out on the left of the picture hung a comet, tiny and remote: and between all and behind all, far more emphatic and palpable than it showed on Earth, the undimensioned, enigmatic blackness. The lights trembled: they seemed to grow brighter as he looked. Stretched naked on his bed, a second Danaë, he found it night by night more difficult to disbelieve in old astrology: almost he felt, wholly he imagined, "sweet influence" pouring or even stabbing into his surrendered body. (OSP, 28)

Bedford had reacted in much the same way. Thus, his sense of disembodiment (an old convention of the cosmic voyage):

It was the strangest sensation conceivable, floating thus loosely in space, at first indeed horribly strange, and when the horror passed, not disagreeable at all, exceedingly restful! Indeed the nearest thing in earthly experience to it that I know is lying on a very thick soft feather bed. But the quality of utter detachment and independence! I had not reckoned on anything like this. I had expected a violent jerk at starting, a giddy sense of speed. Instead I felt—as if I were disembodied. It was not like the beginning of a journey; it was like the beginning of a dream.[6]

Or Mr. Bedford's first sight of the stars, now seen from outside Earth's atmosphere:

There came a click and then a window in the outer case yawned open. The sky outside was as black as the darkness within the sphere, but the shape of the open window was marked by an infinite number of stars.

Those who have seen the starry sky only from the earth cannot imagine its appearance when the vague half-luminous veil of our air has been withdrawn. The stars we see on earth are the mere scattered survivors that penetrate our misty atmosphere. But now at last I could realise the meaning of the hosts of heaven! Stranger things were presently to see, but that airless, stardusted sky! Of all things I think that will be one of the last I shall forget.[7]

Malacandra (Mars) is, I think, the best imaginary world in space ever to appear in fiction. It is a step beyond what Wells does so well in *The First Men in the Moon*, and, in case there is any doubt as to Lewis's intent, we have his own statements about what he was doing. The idea, though none of the details, came from David Lindsay's *A Voyage to Arcturus*. Writing about Lindsay's book in "On Stories," Lewis said,

> There is no recipe for writing of this kind. But part of the secret is that the author (like Kafka) is recording a lived dialectic. His Tormance is a region of the spirit. He is the first writer to discover what "other planets" are really good for in fiction. No merely physical strangeness or merely spatial distance will realize that idea of otherness which is what we are always trying to grasp in a story about voyaging through space: you must go into another dimension. To construct plausible and moving "other worlds" you must draw on the only real "other world" we know, that of the spirit.[8]

He said much the same thing in a letter: "I had grown up on Wells's stories of that kind; it was Lindsay who first gave me the idea that the 'scientifiction' appeal could be combined with the 'supernatural' appeal. . . ."[9] The "other dimension" of spirit which Lewis adds is to make Malacandra an unfallen world. But the success of Lewis's portrayal of another world is hardly dependent on this other dimension of spirit. Malacandra is also a world carefully worked out in its physical details and ecology.

Miss Nicolson is probably right in seeing in Malacandra elements of Keplerian terror, but mostly, I think, it is a representative—probably the best—of the Martian romance. We have Lewis's own admission on this point in his essay, "On Science Fiction."

> When I myself put canals on Mars I believe I already knew that better telescopes had dissipated that old optical

delusion. The point was that they were part of the Martian myth as it already existed in the common mind.[10]

Impetus for the myth of the superior Martians came in 1877, when Giovanni Schiaparelli made his sensational discovery of the canals of Mars. Observing our neighbor world from the clear atmosphere of Milan, the Italian astronomer found that what had been taken for continents were actually areas separated by straight lines, which he called *canali* because he thought they were "grooves" in the planet's surface. The Italian word was mistranslated as *canals,* and the supposed existence of artificial waterways immediately suggested life on the planet, an idea to which the public responded with enthusiasm.

Although professional astronomers in the 1880's and 1890's were reluctant to accept the canals, a few scientists like Percival Lowell developed elaborate theories about life on Mars, which they thought were proved by the existence of the canals. The main element in these theories was the concept that Mars was an aging world much older than Earth. The nebular hypothesis helped support such a conclusion, for a planet like Mars, further from the Sun, must have been created before our world. In addition, Mars was smaller than Earth, and the cooling and subsequent development of the planet could have proceeded more rapidly. If, as seemed likely, life had begun ages earlier on Mars, then it would have had time to evolve to higher levels than on Earth. The great system of canals indicated that the inhabitants of Mars were indeed far-advanced, for only beings much superior to men could have constructed the planet-spanning network which had been observed.

Perhaps the most fully developed explanation of the conditions on Mars was given by the American astronomer Lowell, who believed that Mars was not only an older world but a world nearing death. In his very widely read *Mars* (1895) and in subsequent books and articles, Lowell found the greatest threat to life on the planet to be the diminishing supply of water, which, retreating through cracks and caverns into the interior, had emptied oceans, seas, and lakes. Since the water supply was scarce, he reasoned that there was but one course open to the inhabitants of Mars in order to support life: "Irrigation, and upon as vast a scale as possible, must be the all-engrossing Martian pursuit." Lowell believed that the Martians had united into a supra-national community to perform the tremendous engineering feat of constructing the planet-wide canal system, which carried water from the melting polar caps to the desert regions, and he concluded that the Martians had to be politically, socially, and technologically far advanced. Without doubt the Martians possessed machines of which we had not even dreamed, and with them such inventions as the telephone and motion pictures were things of a bygone past, "preserved with veneration in museums as relics of the clumsy contrivances of the simple childhood of the race."

Details of this advanced Martian world were filled in by writers of fiction, who expanded the idea that the Martians had harnessed the forces of nature to build a civilization as yet undreamed of on Earth. From the 1880's to the 1930's, numerous stories were written on this theme and its important variant, the invasion from Mars—the two best in the latter category being Kurd Lasswitz's *Auf zwei Planeten* and Wells's *The War of the Worlds*. The viability of the Martian myth as late as 1938 can be seen in the popular reaction to Orson Welles's radio dramatization of *The War of the Worlds*. Lewis's *Out of the Silent Planet* in the same year lifted the Martian myth to a very high level as literature.

Malacandra, brilliantly the Mars of the myth, is seen through the eyes of a frightened Ransom (he had overheard a conversation on ship between Weston and Devine, which revealed their intention of turning him over to the inhabitants of Malacandra). The sense of alienness begins with his first look out the manhole: "Naturally enough all he saw was the ground—a circle of pale pink, almost of white: whether very close and short vegetation or very wrinkled and granulated rock or soil he could not say." Lewis employs a clever piece of psychological insight for the controlling principle of Ransom's impressions: "Moreover, he knew nothing yet well enough to see it: you cannot see things till you know roughly what they are."

It is only gradually that he comes to learn the nature of the new world, for at first everything is vague and unfocused: "a great, brilliantly cumular mass of rose colour"; "a bright, pale world—a water-colour world out of a child's paint box"; "a flat belt of light blue." Soon he recognizes the blue as water, but his perceptions are still blurred.

A mass of something purple, so huge that he took it for a heather-covered mountain, was his first impression: on the other side, beyond the larger water, there was something of the same kind. But there, he could see over the top of it. Beyond were strange upright shapes of whitish green: too jagged and irregular for buildings, too thin and steep for mountains. Beyond and above these again was the rose-coloured cloud-like mass. It might really be a cloud, but it was very solid-looking and did not seem to have moved since he first set eyes on it from the manhole. It looked like the top of a gigantic red cauliflower—or like a huge bowl of red soapsuds—and it was exquisitely beautiful in tint and shape. (OSP, 42)

Then he masters another detail.

The purple stuff was vegetation: more precisely it was vegetables, vegetables about twice the height of English elms, but apparently soft and flimsy. The stalks—one could hardly call them trunks—rose smooth and round, and surprisingly thin, or about forty feet: above that, the huge plants opened into a sheaf-like development, not of branches but of leaves, leaves as large as lifeboats but nearly transparent. The whole thing corresponded roughly to his idea of a submarine forest: the plants, at once so large and so frail, seemed to need water to support them, and he wondered that they could hang in the air. Lower down, between the stems, he saw the vivid purple twilight, mottled with paler sunshine, which made up the internal scenery of the wood. (OSP, 42–43)

Not long after this a group of *sorns* (one of the intelligent species of Malacandra) comes to greet them; and, overwhelmed with fright, Ransom escapes from his captors. And so, on his own, as the first crushing fear wears off, Ransom begins to discover significant details about the new world. One of the first is the theme of perpendicularity:

> As he continued crossing ridges and gullies he was struck with their extreme steepness; but somehow they were not very difficult to cross. He noticed, too, that even the smallest hummocks of earth were of an unearthly shape—too narrow, too pointed at the top and too small at the base. He remembered that the waves on the blue lakes had displayed a similar oddity. And glancing up at the purple leaves he saw the same theme of perpendicularity—the same rush to the sky—repeated there. (*OSP*, 47)

He has "sufficient science" to guess that he is on a smaller world with lesser gravitation (the effects of the different gravity of another world are a necessary detail in every cosmic voyage), though it isn't until later in his stay that he realizes he is on Mars. Another early discovery is that the blue water which hisses down streams into the lakes must come from some hotter subterranean source. After spending a day and a night alone, he is befriended by one of the *hrossa*, another of the intelligent species of Malacandra, and from then on he quickly sheds his fear and comes rapidly to know about the new world.

What he comes to learn is that it is the older, dying world of the Martian myth. The surface is desert and vast red petrified forest—uninhabited because of the cold and the thinness of the air. All of the life of the planet is to be found in or along the great long canals—actually deep canyons (called *handramit*)—where there is warmth, water, and air to breathe. The *harandra*—the surface—is as barren and desolate: "jagged peaks blazing in sunlight against an almost black sky." At one point Ransom is taken on a journey near the limits of the atmosphere, in order to cross from one *handramit* to another. It is an awesome sight, a world of naked, faintly greenish rock, interrupted with wide patches of red, extended to the horizon. The heaven, darkest blue where the rock met it, was almost black at the zenith, and looking in any direction where sunlight did not blind him, he could see the stars. (*OSP*, 106)

And he gets a close look at the petrified forests.

Over the edge of the valley, as if it had frothed down from the true *harandra*, came great curves of the rose-tinted, cumular stuff which he had seen so often from a distance. Now on a nearer view they appeared hard as stone in substance, but puffed above and stalked beneath like vegetation. His original simile of giant cauliflower turned out to be surprisingly correct—stone cauliflowers the size of cathedrals and the colour of pale rose. (*OSP*, 107)

His guide explains that once "there was air on the *harandra* and it was warm." Great forests grew, and "in and out among their stalks" went a people who glided through the air on "broad flat limbs." "It is said they were great singers, and in those days the red forests echoed with their music" (*OSP*, 107).

Finally, a last look at Malacandra as the spaceship returns to the Earth reveals the Mars of Percival Lowell's drawings:

Each minute more *handramits* came into view—long straight lines, some parallel, some intersecting, some building triangles. The landscape became increasingly geometrical. The waste between the purple lines appeared perfectly flat. The rosy colour of the petrified forests accounted for its tint immediately below him; but to the north and east the great sand deserts of which the *sorns* had told him were now appearing as illimitable stretches of yellow and ochre. To the west a huge discolouration began to show. It was an irregular patch of greenish blue that looked as if it were sunk below the level of the surrounding *harandra*. He concluded it was the forest lowland of the *pfifltriggi*—or rather one of their forest lowlands, for now similar patches were appearing in all directions, some of them mere blobs at the intersection of *handramits*, some of them of vast extent. (*OSP*, 150)

He muses on how much he never learned about Mars, such as the gigantic feat of engineering involved in the digging of the *handramits* ages before.

In portraying the three rational species (or *hnau*) of Malacandra, Lewis carries the myth of the advanced Martians to its ultimate. He has Wells very much in mind, as is apparent in the famous passage early in *Out of the Silent Planet*, where Ransom speculates on what the inhabitants of the world to which he is being taken will be like.

> His mind, like so many minds of his generation, was richly furnished with bogies. He had read his H. G. Wells and others. His universe was peopled with horrors such as ancient and medieval mythology could hardly rival. No insect-like, vermiculate or crustacean Abominable, no twitching feelers, rasping wings, slimy coils, curling tentacles, no monstrous union of superhuman intelligence and insatiable cruelty seemed to him anything but likely on an alien world. (*OSP*, 33)

There are other places where this idea is expressed: "His whole imaginative training somehow encouraged him to associate superhuman intelligence with monstrosity of form and ruthlessness of will" (*OSP*, 60). Lewis is remembering the Selenites of *The First Men in the Moon*—insect-like creatures—and the Martians of *The War of the Worlds*—men after a million years more of evolution, who are merely giant brains with tentacle-like hands.

In answer to this conception of the inhabitants of another world, Lewis creates his unfallen Malacandra, whose *hnau* are indeed superior as the Martian myth demanded—but what a twist! They are morally and spiritually superior, not scientifically and technologically (though when needed they have very advanced scientific knowledge at their command).

Lewis is extraordinarily successful in portraying the rationality and goodness of the three species of *hnau*: the *hrossa*, the *sorns*, and the *pfifltriggi* (there are also other beings, the *eldila*, who, though they have a material existence of a sort, are what we would call spirits or angels).

In the *hrossa*, Malacandra's theme of perpendicularity is also carried out: they are six or seven feet high and, by earthly standards, too tall for their size. They are curious looking creatures indeed, "a coat of thick black hair, lucid as seal-skin, very short legs with webbed feet, a broad beaver-like or fish-like tail, strong forelimbs with webbed claws or fingers. . . ." A *hross*, Ransom decided,

> was something like a penguin, something like an otter, something like a seal; the slenderness and flexibility of the body suggested a giant stoat. The great round head, heavily whiskered, was mainly responsible for the suggestion of seal; but it was higher in the forehead than a seal's and the mouth was smaller. (*OSP*, 55)

In the *hrossa*, whom Ransom comes to love after he has thrown off his initial fear of alien creatures, we see what men might have been had Paradise never been lost. Naturally continent and monogamous, never overbreeding or exceeding their supply of food, they do not kill other *hnau*; neither do they covet each other's property. Instead, they lead simple, pastoral lives free from the anxieties of a technologically complex civilization, and they die without fear, knowing there is a life to come. They are the great poets and singers of Malacandra.

The *sorns* are more grotesque, more like the popular expectation in the 1930's of what a Martian would be: they suggest one of Frank R. Paul's covers for the early pulp science-fiction magazines (Lewis was, of course, an avid reader of these magazines). "Stalky, flexible-looking distortions of earthly bipeds," they are "twice or three times the height of man," "crazily thin and elongated in the leg," "top-heavily pouted in the chest." Their faces are long and drooping, their heads narrow and conical, their hands "thin, mobile, spidery, and almost transparent." They speak with enormous horn-like voices. At first Ransom is horrified at the sight of them, thinking of them as "ogres"; later, when he gets to know them, he decides that "Titans" or "Angels" would be a better word. The intellectuals of Mars, they are astonished at what Ransom has to tell them of "human history—of war, slavery, and prostitition." At one point they show Ransom his Earth through a telescope: "It was the bleakest moment in all his travels."

We learn little about the third species of *hnau*, the *pfifltriggi*. They are frog-like creatures who are the artists and craftsmen of Mars and almost as foolish as men in their love of *things*: the more useless or the more complicated an object, the more its creation interests them. But, of course, they are better than men; their concept of work —something one does because he loves it—puts us to shame.

The climax of Lewis's contrast of Earthly and Malacandrian life comes in the scene before the Oyarsa when Weston—he and Devine have been captured after killing three of the *hrossa*—extols the superiority of Earthly civilization. Weston, a man obsessed with the idea that the human species, at all cost, must contrive to seed itself throughout the universe, insists upon man's right to supersede the Malacandrians as the right of the higher over the lower. "Your tribal life, with its stone-age weapons and beehive huts, its primitive coracles and elementary social structure," he tells the Oyarsa, "has nothing to compare with our civilization, with our science, medicine and law, our armies, our architecture, our commerce, and our transport." Just how superior this civilization really is Lewis makes clear by the technique of having Ransom attempt to translate Weston's speech—Weston speaks Malacandrian very badly—for the Oyarsa. Translated into the language of an unfallen world, Weston's praise of earthly science, medicine and law, armies, architecture, commerce, and transportation sounds like this:

> He [Weston] says we know much. There is a thing happens in our world when the body of a living creature feels pain and becomes weak, and he says we sometimes know how to stop it. He says we have many bent people [Malacandrian for criminals] and we kill them or shut them in huts and that we have people for settling quarrels between the bent *hnau* about their huts and mates and

things. He says we have many ways for the *hnau* of one land to kill those of another and some are trained to it. He says we build very big and strong huts of stones and other things—like the *pfifltriggi*. And he says we exchange many things among ourselves and carry heavy weights very quickly a long way. Because of all this, he says it would not be the act of a bent *hnau* if our people killed all your people. (*OSP*, 147)

In the context of the novel, this denunciation of earthly life—or perhaps, more accurately, Western civilization—is extremely effective. There is added interest in the fact that in its entirety the interview with the Oyarsa is a splendid continuation of the long tradition which begins with Gulliver's interview with the King of Brobdingnag (and includes, of course, Cavor's with the Grand Lunar). In all fairness, though, one should also note that Lewis's judgment on human life (taken together with his other values expressed in the whole of the trilogy) would by some be considered unfair and biased. Robert Conquest has even gone as far as seeing Lewis, along with Charles Williams, as representing the totalitarian mind; and whatever the truth of that accusation, certainly the trilogy is in large part an attack on the Wellsian sort of scientific materialism and utopianism.[11] *Out of the Silent Planet*, however, is the least propagandistic of the three volumes in the trilogy. When certain contemporary currents of intellectual feeling and thought, which tend to find something congenial in Lewis's philosophy, have run their course—and when certain tastes in literary criticism have had their day—then I think *Out of the Silent Planet* may well be valued ahead of the other two books. It should then be valued for just what it is: the last and best (or second best) example of that minor genre of fantasy, the cosmic voyage.

"Now Entertain Conjecture of a Time" — The Fictive Worlds of C. S. Lewis and J. R. R. Tolkien

J. R. R. Tolkien's "On Fairy-Stories," the essay that best explains the author's conception of the genre of *The Lord of the Rings*, was delivered as one of the Andrew Lang Lectures at St. Andrews in 1938; [1] the corresponding, though hardly derivative, exposition by C. S. Lewis of the form and meaning of the "Fantastic or Mythical" as a genre and of the genesis of the Narnia books, "Sometimes Fairy Stories May Say Best What's to be Said," appeared in the Children's Book Section of the *New York Times Book Review* for November 18, 1956 (p. 3). Although Lewis had presumably held the ideas presented there for years, this short essay echoes many of the crucial points of the Tolkien essay—that the fairy story is a legitimate form of fiction having its own set of means and ends; that it is not in any way the exclusive property of children; that it has its origins not in abstractions or ideas or personifications or allegories, but in a set of images searching for a form, which in time becomes, through art, a whole sub-creation having the inner consistency of reality—and in doing so bears witness to the fundamental agreement between the two men as to the integrity and high seriousness of the mythmaking genre in which both are writing.

In the *New York Times* article, however, Lewis makes a comment about the Narnia books which, as far as I can discover, has no exact parallel in any of Tolkien's statements and which serves in spite of the similarity of the two essays to separate rather drastically the aims of the two writers. Having discussed the origin of the Narnia series in a set of images—"a faun carrying an umbrella, a queen on a sledge, a magnificent lion"—which "sorted themselves into events" and eventually into the form of the fairy tale, Lewis goes on to assert that in the process of creation the moral concerns of the "author as man, citizen or Christian" came to dominate the initial creative impulses of the "author as author" and so determined the specifically Christian nature and purpose of the work in hand.

> I thought I saw how stories of this kind [the Narnia books] could steal past a certain inhibition which had paralyzed much of my own religion in childhood. . . . The whole subject was associated with lowered voices; almost as if it were something medical. But supposing that by casting all these things into an imaginary world, stripping them of their stained-glass and Sunday school associations, one could make them for the first time appear in their real potency.

Thus, although beginning with images which developed into a literary form, the seven books became rather deliberately, if not allegories, then at least deliberate expositions of the great articles of the Christian faith, the Trinity, the Creation of the world through the agency of the Son, Original Sin, the Atonement, Repentance and Rebirth, the Second Coming, the Final Judgment—all are presented, stripped "of their stained-glass and Sunday school associations," in the tales of Aslan and the Pevensie children, who themselves represent the various sorts and conditions of Christian men: capable, honorable Peter, feminine Susan, self-centered Edmund, and saintly Lucy.

Such a clearly didactic purpose and method appear never to have occurred to Tolkien. Quite the opposite, in fact. The usual explanations of the genesis of *The Lord of the Rings*—that he wrote the tales in order to use the language and the history (Tolkien's equivalent of Lewis's images) or that they lay within him for years "like a great tumor" [2] —certainly indicate no didactic purpose such as that which moved Lewis, and the accounts of its slow, measured growth by Tolkien and his friends demonstrate clearly enough that tale and meaning grew together inseparably in the author's mind during the process of creation.

Thus Lewis in the Narnia books set out to teach a set of doctrines and Tolkien in *The Lord of the Rings* to— who knows what exactly?—perhaps simply to create, to use his own terms, a Fantasy, and through Fantasy, the Recovery of a "clear view" of life, an Escape from the burdens and limitations of existence, and a Consolation (*The Tolkien Reader*, pp. 46 ff.). On the question of the creative means to their ends, however, the two are in firm agreement. Mere narrative, however complex and exciting, is not enough. The means either to Christian indoctrination or to Recovery, Escape, and Consolation, the "trick," as Dorothy Sayers calls it,[3] of all successful fiction is particularity, the ability to create and sustain a whole sub-creation. As Lewis says, "the *plot* . . . is only really a net whereby to catch something else. The real theme may be, and perhaps usually is, something . . . much more like a state or quality" [4] —in short, the whole created milieu against and in which the plot unfolds itself, the created world which gives substance, particularity, and hence the truth of experience, however vicarious, to a work of art.

It is no surprise, therefore, to find Tolkien and Lewis creating with such care and enthusiasm their own fictional worlds in order to provide the kind of substantive background both thought necessary to fiction. It is possible to reconstruct a history and geography of Narnia from the books alone, and even without the maps and genealogical tables the terrain and families of Middle-earth are as clear to us as those of London or Boston or Yoknapatawpha County, "William Faulkner, sole owner and proprietor." [5]

Despite their similarity in intent, however, the created worlds of Tolkien and Lewis differ in character in a way that reveals sharply the separate literary intentions of their owners and proprietors. Simply stated, Narnia is essentially Christian and Middle-earth essentially pagan in conception, or, better said, Narnia is the kind of world in which Christian concepts may be translated into events and Middle-earth from which heroic patterns may evolve. The whole history of Narnia from its creation in *The Magician's Nephew* to its final judgment and transformation in *The Last Battle* is structured by the optimistic Christian pattern of fall and redemption, and each of the individual novels follows a similar theological design in which sin and evil are overcome by the children acting on behalf of Aslan. *The Lord of the Rings*, on the other hand, is in no way theological either in its structure or in its thematic pattern. Middle-earth, or at least certain portions of it, is the stark, basically pessimistic world of the sagas in which God does not intervene in human conflicts and in which the hero's or the society's struggle against evil culminates at best in a temporary victory achieved at tremendous cost.

I would maintain that the two world-views, in spite of the shared Christianity of their authors, are opposed in kind and, furthermore, that it is impossible to construct an heroic poem—heroic, that is, in the traditional literary sense—that is at the same time Christian. For despite all recent criticism to the contrary, *Beowulf* is not basically a Christian poem, although its author was himself doubtless so persuaded. And *The Song of Roland*, in spite of its constant professions of the rightness of the Christian code, is in spirit and ethos as brutally pagan as any Viking war cry.

For Christian values, theologically considered at least, are opposed to heroic ones. The doctrine of the forgiveness of sins, if nothing else, strictly followed prohibits revenge and the vendetta, concepts which are a part of nearly all heroic poetry. More important, the Christian view of life is unflaggingly optimistic. God will eventually turn evil to good, and even the tortured heroes of Graham Greene emerge triumphant (at least in Christian terms) over the godless secularism of contemporary society. The world inhabited by the epic hero is, on the other hand, basically a tormented battle ground, a darkling plain in which confused armies clash by night and in which there is no assurance that God has taken sides at all, in which evil must be combatted simply because it is a part of the heroic code to do so, and in which, although the hero may gain a temporary victory, his eventual defeat is both expected and acknowledged.

In spite of Tolkien's own implication in "On Fairy-Stories" that *The Lord of the Rings*, ending as it does in a "sudden, joyous 'turn'" (p. 68) (and surely no one would deny that it does so end), possesses eucatastrophe and is hence by extension both optimistic and Christian, I would maintain that the book itself does not bear out this view and that it reflects the attitudes and interests of Tolkien the student of *Beowulf* rather than those of Tolkien the Christian. The chronicles of the First and Second Ages, presented by allusions in *The Lord of the Rings* proper and in the annals comprising Appendices A and B in *The Return of the King*,[6] are filled with accounts of never-ceasing wars against evil waged by dwarves, elves, hobbits, and men and of the reappearance in every age of the forces of darkness. The heroic elves and men of the First Age manage with the help of the *silmaril* to defeat Morgoth, "The Great Enemy, of whom Sauron of Mordor was but a servant," but "Beren [who had stolen the *silmaril* from the very crown of Morgoth] was slain by the Wolf that came from the gates of Angband" and Lúthien, his elven wife, chose mortality "so that she might follow him" (I, 206). In the Second Age, the Númenorean kings, descendents of Lúthien, under the influence of Sauron attempt to gain immortality by conquering the Undying Lands and are destroyed. And although Sauron loses his bodily form in the destruction of Númenor, his spirit escapes to Middle-earth where he wars against the remnants of the Númenoreans. Here he is defeated again and the One Ring taken from him at the end of the Second Age, but in the next thousand years he rebuilds his empire of evil which is only finally destroyed by the Ring Companions in the War of the Rings.

Nor is this the end of evil in Middle-earth, though Tolkien's chronicles do not extend into the Fourth Age. For the Fourth Age is that of Men, and its history is all too familiar to us. Dwarves have been "abandoned to folk-tales" or to "nonsense-stories in which they have become mere figures of fun" (III, 415); elves "dwell now beyond the circles of the world, and do not return" (III, 416); the hobbits have retreated under their hills and "they avoid us with dismay and are becoming hard to find" (I, 11). The very disappearance from Middle-earth of these creatures of a simpler, and essentially more heroic, past bears witness to the continuing influence of Sauron, under whatever name, in the Age of Men. In a sense, *Beowulf*, in which the old values still hold, is the first document of the Fourth Age and *The Trial* its contemporary ledger.

What is true of civilizations in the Tolkien saga is true also of their heroes. Though the forces of good triumph in each age, their leaders pay a high cost for victory. In the First Age, Beren escapes the forces of the great Enemy and "through great peril came over the Mountains of Terror" (I, 206). He is later parted from Lúthien and cast into the dungeons of Sauron. Finally he is killed by the "Wolf that came from the gates of Angband," and the widowed Lúthien chooses mortality and death in order to join her husband.

In the Second Age, Elendil and his sons manage to escape the general downfall of Númenor only to be besieged again by Sauron, whom they believed they had destroyed. The Last Alliance succeeds finally in defeating Sauron, but in the battle Elendil is slain and the Great Ring taken from Sauron by Isildur, who refuses to destroy it and is finally slain at Gladden Fields. Elrond himself, in fact, declares the victory of the Last Alliance to be "fruitless," since in spite of the sacrifices of Gil-galad and Elendil "Sauron was diminished, but not destroyed. His Ring was lost but not unmade" (I, 257). And he goes on to lament the evils that have befallen Middle-earth in the Third Age.

/ The tragic effects of the struggle against evil are seen throughout *The Lord of the Rings*, particularly in Frodo. At first an innocent hobbit, he is drawn into the war against Sauron against his will: "I am not made for perilous quests," he protests. "I wish I had never seen the Ring! Why did it come to me? Why was I chosen?" (I, 70). And as the quest proceeds, the Ring begins to work its terrible magic upon him, weakening his will and gradually destroying his faith in his mission, until, almost like Gollum, he becomes "enslaved to that Ring, unable to find peace or relief ever in life again" (III, 222). In the end, he has to be dragged to his destiny by Sam, who alone has retained the innocence of the Shire, and at the very last, he almost fails to destroy the Ring: "I will not do this deed. The Ring is mine!" he cries out atop Mount Doom (III, 223), and he, and Middle-earth, are finally saved only by a greed for the Ring greater than his own, that of Gollum.

Nor does Frodo ever recover from his experience; the scars cannot be erased even by victory. During the journey back to the Shire, Gandalf replies to Frodo's statement that his "wound [received from the Ringwraiths] aches, and the memory of darkness is heavy" upon him that "there are some wounds that cannot be wholly cured" (III, 268). Just before his passing, Frodo tells Sam that he has been "deeply hurt": "I tried to save the Shire," he continues, "and it has been saved, but not for me. It must often be so, Sam, when things are in danger: some one has to give them up, lose them, so that others may keep them" (III, 309).

The views of nature and civilization, like those of history and the individual life, advanced in *The Lord of the Rings* seem also be pagan rather than Christian in essence. There is no hearkening back, as there is in the Narnia books, to a Golden Age when Adam delved and Eve span in the perfect innocence and ease of an uncorrupted nature, and the memory of Treebeard, the Ent, cannot extend beyond a time when the "Great Darkness" did not exist somewhere. Even the innocence of the Shire, which has to be maintained by the constant vigilance of the Rangers, is marred by internal family bickerings, and once one leaves the Shire, he is thrown into the dangers of a malevolent nature. The "bad-hearted" trees of the Old Forest seek to destroy him; the fogs of the Barrow-downs and the storms and crags of the Misty Mountain deter his journey; orcs, trolls, the great spider Shelob everywhere lie in wait for him. The very place names east of the Brandywine bespeak the dread that surrounds the region: the Mountain of Shadow, the Haunted Pass, the Dead Marshes, the Mere of Dead Faces, Mount Doom. As in the pagan heroic literature of the West, civilization is seen in terms of outposts, little circles of light and fellowship dotting the forests of the night—"The Prancing Pony," Barliman Butterbur's inn at Bree, Tom Bombadil's house, and Rivendell, "The Last Homely House east of the Sea." Finally the little circles of light die out altogether, and there are no more havens, only the wastes and mountains of Mordor.

To come to the Narnia volumes from *The Lord of the Rings* is to enter a gayer, happier world. Lewis is committed, in advance, to a Christian point of view, and his Christianity everywhere dictates not only his choice of incident and character, such as the patently allegorical presentation of Aslan's "crucifixion" in *The Lion, the Witch and the Wardrobe*, but also the very structure of the fictional world he is involved in creating.

The Lion, the Witch and the Wardrobe, the first of the Narnia series to be written and the prototype of those that follow it, shows these differences well enough. Narnia is essentially a spoiled Eden, a snow-bound garden, not like Middle-earth a hideous complex of forests, marshes, and mountains made habitable only by the unceasing efforts of men, hobbits, dwarves, and elves. In the Narnia series, sin and evil come to Earth through Man—represented in *The Magician's Nephew* by the introduction of the white witch, Jadis, into the new world by the children at the moment of its creation—and the Pevensie children, under the direction of Aslan, are involved in each book in the struggle to free the land from its evil enchantment and to return it to its former garden state. In *The Lord of the Rings*, on the other hand, the forces of civilization are seen as attempting to order a basically disordered and chaotic creation, not as trying to restore a lost golden age.

Hence the inhabitants of Narnia do what those of Middle-earth never do: they reminisce about the "good old days," "about the midnight dances and how the Nymphs who lived in the wells and the Dryads who lived in the trees came out to dance with the Fauns." [7] And since all creation has descended from these innocent, idyllic days, there are no intrinsically evil creatures at large in Narnia as it appears in *The Lion, the Witch and the Wardrobe*—no Shelobs, orcs, or trolls. The "Cruels and Hags and Incubuses, Wraiths, Horrors, Efretts, Sprites, Orknies, Wooses, and Ettins" (p. 140) that accompany Jadis are brought from outside and are killed by the children and by the true animal inhabitants of Narnia, who have been turned to stone by the White Witch and are returned to their rightful state by Aslan.

Beginning with *Prince Caspian*, however, fallen animals, the Narnian equivalents of fallen men, do appear, and it is my guess that Lewis has here slightly altered his original concept of Narnia in order to present the doctrine of Original Sin. In each of the later novels, the forces of evil are seen, in accordance with Augustinian doctrine, as attempting to pervert in some manner the natural, inherent God-given goodness of the Narnian animals, either by suppressing any knowledge of Aslan as in *Prince Caspian* or by brainwashing techniques (much like those used in *That Hideous Strength*) in *The Silver Chain* and *The Last Battle*. Evil thus always comes from outside Narnia, from Charu or Calormen or Telnar; it is not inherent in either the nature or the inhabitants of Narnia as it is in those of Middle-earth.

The effect of evil upon the protagonists of good serves

also to define the differences between the Christian world of Lewis and the heroic one of Tolkien. As we have seen, the heroes of the Tolkien saga are able to achieve their victories over their antagonists only at considerable personal cost. Lewis's heroes, on the other hand, emerge unscathed from their trials. True, Edmund in *The Lion, the Witch and the Wardrobe* emerges as a "graver and quieter man than Peter" (p. 169) and Lucy follows what Charles Williams called the "Way of Negation," but there is no indication that Lewis's heroes are maimed in body and disheartened in spirit as is Frodo. They instead emerge from their trials happily victorious, are duly praised and rewarded, and, filled with a sense of having fulfilled the desires of Aslan, return to their homes in England.

It is impossible, however, to describe adequately the major difference between the created worlds of Narnia and Middle-earth, that of tone. The presence of the children in the Narnia series does much of course to lighten the tone of the Narnia books; one cannot very well imagine a child-protagonist in *Beowulf* or the *Nibelungenlied*. But the necessity of adhering to Christian doctrine, to its view of a redeemable mankind and nature, everywhere simplifies character and lightens incident. Considered as a cycle, the Narnia books work toward the final salvation of all nature at the Final Judgment of Narnia in *The Last Battle*, the happiest of all eucatastrophic endings. *The Lord of the Rings*, on the other hand, ends with the bittersweet departure from Middle-earth of the Ring Companions, but also with prophecies of struggle and sorrow to come. There is no undiluted joy, no pure eucatastrophe in Tolkien, in spite of the "beat and lifting of the heart" (*The Tolkien Reader*, p. 69) which accompany its final pages. The adjectives which one finds most suitable to describe the tone of the Narnia books—*charming, graceful, fanciful, serene*—simply do not apply to *The Lord of the Rings*; *roughhewn, rugged, heroic*, and, finally, *splendid* seem more appropriate to Tolkien.

Lewis's admitted purpose in writing the Narnia stories

—the propagation of the Faith—can thus be seen to determine the kind of fictional world he has created. Tolkien, beginning perhaps only with a desire to recover the lost simplicity of a world in which we might "be startled anew (but not blinded) by blue and yellow and red" (*The Tolkien Reader,* p. 57), has on the other hand framed a world in which the older and simpler values of the heroic age may function naturally, unencumbered by the sophisticated structures of a time when street-lamps somehow seem more real than trees. C. S. Lewis, by his own statement, in the end came to regard the purposes of the man, in his case the Christian, as being superior to those of the artist. Tolkien, I think, did not, and if *The Lord of the Rings* thus seems more pagan than Christian, it is in this way a tribute to the artistry of a man whose essential thought is closer to that of the Althing than to that of the councils of the Vatican and who has thus created a work which "moves in our northern world beneath our northern sky, and for those who are native to that tongue and land, it must ever call with a profound appeal—until the dragon comes."[8]

Meaning in *The Lord of the Rings*

CLYDE S. KILBY

I should like to suggest several ways in which the *Rings* seems to make its bid as a creation of permanent value.

To begin with, it provides a dependable realization of time. Almost from the beginning we learn not merely of the quaint genealogies of the Bagginses and Boffins, the Tooks and Brandybucks, but in a serious vein we begin to discover the long history of the Elven-rings, and the perils of owning one of the Rings of Power. Leaving the Shire, Bilbo says, "The Road goes ever on and on," a prospect that gains significance by retrospect. Ancestry and antiquity are everywhere manifest and a viable history buttresses every point of decision. There are direct allusions to, as well as a constant almost magical intuition of, previous transpirations. Hobbits, elves, dwarves, men, and even orcs have a regard for history. Departing from the Grey Havens, Frodo exhorts Sam, as the Fourth Age of Middle-earth begins, to keep reading things out of the Red Book so as to retain the memory of previous ages.

The *Rings* is a world and one containing its own myths and legends from the immemorial past. The star most loved by the elves is that of Eärendil, the mariner who long before had made his perilous way from Middle-earth to Valinor and there heard things too sacred for mortal lands and therefore was set to sail his ship as a star.[1] The past often comes with enchantment pervaded with meaning as did the songs of the elves at Rivendell to Frodo, when it seemed the "words took shape, and visions of far lands and bright things . . . opened out before him; and the firelit hall became like a golden mist above seas of foam that sighed upon the margins of the world . . . until he felt that an endless river of swelling gold and silver was flowing over him." [2] This was the kind of experience that had the practical effect of arming a modest hobbit for the perils ahead.

More interesting, some of the best-loved characters come to us literally alive from the ancient past. Tom Bombadil is "oldest and fatherless," and he remembers when the sun was young. Treebeard is almost as old. Galadriel is one of the Eldar and vastly older than the 6462 years of the First and Second Ages. Sauron was the greatest of the servants of Melkor in the First Age.

And strikingly enough, it is a world in which myths turn out to be true. When today ninety-nine out of a hundred people regard myths as utter make-believe, one can imagine the shock of discovering not Martians but the god Mars himself in the land. When everybody knows that the sun is "merely" vast heat, gases and other elements discoverable by spectroscopic analysis, we can imagine the consternation among us if some great new telescope discovered it to be Helios driving his chariot across the heavens. Stretch the imagination to believe such things and notice what an amazing and larger, and possibly fearful, world we should have. Such was Middle-earth. A universe like ours which has become almost infinitely atomized is a great challenge to the intellect, but the whole man seems to require something more.

Tolkien's friend Owen Barfield has written a number of brilliant books [3] describing a dire process old as civilization, a process in which a world of utter unity, quickened meaning, "divine concreteness," and genuine participation has been slowly replaced by one in which measurement and classified sense perception is dominant. Our world has become emptier and emptier. Today even the intricacies of the human organism and of society appear to be "nothing more than" this or that. No one, I think, has put the situation any better than C. S. Lewis.

At the outset, the universe appears packed with will, intelligence, life and positive qualities; every tree is a nymph and every planet a god. Man himself is akin to the gods. The advance of knowledge gradually empties this rich and genial universe: first of its gods, then of its colours, smells, sounds and tastes, finally of solidity itself as solidity was originally imagined. As these items are taken from the world, they are transferred to the subjective side of the account: classified as our sensations, thoughts, images or emotions. The Subject becomes gorged, inflated, at the expense of the Object. But the matter does not end there. The same method which has emptied the world now proceeds to empty ourselves. The masters of the method soon announce that we were just as mistaken (and mistaken in much the same way) when we attributed "souls," or "selves" or "minds" to human organisms, as when we attributed Dryads to the trees. . . . We, who have personified all other things, turn out to be ourselves mere personifications. . . . And thus we arrive at a result uncommonly like zero. When we were reducing the world to almost nothing we deceived ourselves with the fancy that all its lost qualities were being kept safe (if in a somewhat humbled condition) as "things in our own mind." Apparently we had no mind of the sort required. The Subject is as empty as the Object. Almost nobody has been making linguistic mistakes about almost nothing. By and large, this is the only thing that has ever happened.[4]

I believe that the popularity of the *Rings* is in no small way owing to our need for an entire world rather than an atomized one. Tolkien described the myth-writer as a sub-creator imitating the real Creator and making worlds no less complex yet no less proportioned and hierarchical than His. And such a world appears necessary to our best inner health.

The *Rings* is also epic in scope. When the accounts of the First and Second Age are published, we shall have the record of Middle-earth from its beginning, of rising and crumbling kingdoms, of struggles of natural against natural, supernatural against supernatural, and natural against supernatural, of a vast sweep of events involving thousands of people, and of individual and group heroism — and all within a framework of exalted ethical compass.

Another characteristic of the *Rings* is its noble blending

of melancholy and joy. Not alone is there joy following sorrow temporally, as when the Fellowship sees its leader killed during the fierce struggle in Moria and afterwards finds glorious safety and repose in Lothlórien, but, as in Keats, the sadness often inheres within the joy and beauty. Symbol of the glorious land that has been lost in the West is the unstained one called Lothlórien, the heart of Elvendom on earth, and symbol of Lothlórien's beauty is Galadriel, tall, glorious, white, golden-haired, ageless except for the depth of her eyes. Her song, however, is a sad song of exile and of sorrows that shall be. The whole episode of Lothlórien remains engraven on the page as indelibly as the figures on the Grecian Urn and breaks the heart with the same joy that left Keats pondering on the eternality of beauty and truth. The wedding of Aragorn and Arwen, so long awaited and so glorious, has its sad note in Arwen's renunciation of her Elvish immortality. Even the fond recollections of the hobbits for the distant Shire and comfortable homes has its own small minor tone.

Pleasure unlimited is dissipating but pleasure squeezed out from disaster is keen and salutary. A world presided over by Doom has, nevertheless, its tides of delight. A citizen of Dover described to me the pleasure of a successful journey to and from the grocer's during bombing raids. The poignant moment of Sam's view of the white star while reconnoitering his and Frodo's position in Mordor is one such experience in the *Rings*. The hiatus from danger during the visit to Tom and Goldberry Bombadil's and some of the experiences at Minas Tirith are others. Even the meal of herbs and stewed rabbit provided by Gollum and lovingly prepared by Sam in the dangerous woods of Ithilien refreshes our sense of taste and, far more, our awareness of Sam as the faithful executor of a trust. This joy-in-sorrow atmosphere pervades the *Rings*.

Again, the *Rings* joins the high art of the world in revealing the significance, even the glory, of the ordinary. We need to meet the centaur and the dragon, says Tolkien, in order to open our eyes to horses and dogs and sheep.[5] The walking, talking trees of Fangorn forest have the effect of causing us to note the fantasy of what Tolkien calls "the living tree itself," that is, of trees just at hand.

No book published in recent times creates a more poignant feeling for the essential quality of many outdoor and indoor experiences—of flowing streams and the feel and taste of water, of food when one is desperately hungry, of a pipe and complete relaxation, of being safely shut-in from hurtful forces at the door, of light in dark places, of the coming of dawn, or of the quiet strength of song and legend. After reading the *Rings* one sees and feels more deeply.

Another large factor, I believe, in the success of the *Rings* is its depiction of a world of being as well as of doing. This is perhaps the essential difference between this story and its imitations. Even a mediocre plot-maker often constructs an exciting set of actions, but a world of being is something else. Tolkien's commendation of *Beowulf* as "a composition, not a tune" is applicable to the *Rings*. The main point of the essay on *Beowulf* is not that the dragons are an incongruity but that the poem is defective in its inevitable temptation towards historicism. If that poem has a shortcoming, the difficulty stems basically from inadequacy of imagination. Tolkien has obviously attempted a story without such a flaw. The story-maker, he says, "who allows himself to be 'free with' Nature can be her lover not her slave." [6] The *Rings* is not timid in its conception of character and plot, of intensity and depth. The Ents, for instance, who in a more faltering writer would appear ridiculous, are for Tolkien a triumph. It is something for animals to talk but something greater when trees manage to become fully participating characters.

One of the normal effects of the *Rings* is a reader's wish to turn from the last page back to the first and do it all over again. Mere adventure, such as the detective story, is without this quality. Great writing is always more qualitative than quantitative. Knowing the outcome enhances rather than detracts from the story. It is not simply that Tolkien has spent a lifetime putting his world together but that in all this time the qualities of such a world have been generated and then tested in his creative fires. The apple has come to taste not only of itself but of bud and tree and root and fragrant earthiness itself. So directed and professional is most popular writing today that it is difficult for us to conceive a world seemingly created for its own sake alone, yet under a compulsion as powerful as that of the Ancient Mariner's. As has been said, the story is true to its own inner laws. There is no effort to astonish or to effect any other impression. It is simply "there." Seldom since Defoe has there been such a multitude of concatenating details, particularly in the appendices (an utterly essential part of the story, by the way), with the result that the reader finds it next to impossible, even when not under the spell of the narrative, to believe, for instance, that the Red Book of Westmarch does not exist.

With Tolkien the ordinary notion of fantasy is reversed. A world whose sense of well-being is dictated by exhibitionism, advertising, newspapers and the shoddiness of radio and television is to him a fantastic, not a real world. A world in which newness to the point of eccentricity is the mode and in which styles of music, writing and clothing change fortnightly is to him fantastic. The notion that motor-cars are "more 'real' than, say, horses is pathetically absurd." [7] The real world, on the other hand, is latent and symbolic, where mysteries forever beyond the reach of objective examination meet us on every hand, as indeed they do the great physicists, in such "contemptible" things as matter and light. It is a world in which history is not bunk and truth is a possibility here and now, a world in which God still happens to be alive and man is still responsible, an allusive but not at all an illusive world.

For both Lewis and Tolkien reality begins not in the seen but the unseen. Anything "merely" this or that is likely to be, in an ultimate sense, deceiving. Abstraction of

any sort tends to denigrate the wholeness suggested by
intuition and philosophy and to which images and symbols are an important avenue of understanding. Everything is greater than the sum of its parts. The great
archetypal myth is Christianity (for these men myth is
never antithetical to fact and truth),[8] something respon-
sive to common sense and also to the highest reach of
imagination. Miss Marjorie Wright in her thesis on Lewis,
Tolkien and Charles Williams says that the proper ingredients of myth are timelessness, self-sufficiency (or auton-
omy), and a sense of the numinous.[9] These ingredients
Tolkien finds at the heart of everything good, true and
beautiful. He believes that such ingredients are preserved
to us through myth by the power of imagination. Both
Lewis and Tolkien desire to surmount allegory. Worthy as
that form is, in it a writer puts only what he knows. In
myth he puts more than he knows, what he and his reader
could never come by in any other way. Like Sam's calling
on Elbereth Gilthoniel during his nearly fatal struggle
with Shelob, and like Dimble in *That Hideous Strength*,[10]
he spoke words that are greater and older than himself.
When he is successful, the myth-maker sets forth the
mystery and true reality of the world. Myth takes its place
beside the greatest poetry.

They recognize of course that so far as "conveying a
message" myth has the psychological advantage, if successful, of disarming the reader of his normal inattention and
disbelief. The miracle of art enables a scene or idea to
touch one's full consciousness. A reader totally armored
against anything another man could say may be enticed
into hearing when an elf or a hobbit talks. "Unreality"
becomes the best road to realism. "Admitted fantasy is
precisely the kind of literature which never deceives at
all," says Lewis.[11] A talking tree, a dwarf or an orc is a
creature to listen to naïvely, ingenuously and perhaps
truly.

In addition to his mythmaking gift, or more properly as
a part of it, Tolkien is superbly acquainted with the
pantheon. It is clear that he has not gained his mythic

know-how from dictionaries and handbooks but from touch and hearing, from taste and smell, and from sight better than that of the eyes while meandering in the realms of myth. The high manners, courtesy and strength of purpose in the elves, as indeed the whole atmosphere of the *Rings*, is genuinely blue-blooded. Tolkien writes not in the dubious motive of "giving the people what they want" but in the tradition of great art.

Any writer with a sense of humor is fortunate, since that gift inclines to a sense of balance. Professor Tolkien feels that an ingrained humor is one of his lifelong blessings. A fundamental geniality, and hence of insight, penetrates nearly all he writes. The only instance to the contrary that I recall in his creative works is the satire at the end of the *Rings* on dictators and a materialistic culture. This is for me, in this particular place, an extraneous element and not altogether overcome by the splendid renovative stroke in the regeneration of the Shire and particularly the quick growth of forests by means of Galadriel's magical soil and the springing up of the graceful and golden *mallorn*.

There is no lack of illustration to show that in Tolkien a sense of humor is joined with a good ear. How many of his characters, for instance, promptly identify themselves by the sound of their names: Sam Gamgee, Merry, Pippin, Barliman Butterbur, the Bagginses and the Bolgers and the Fallohides, Fatty Lumpkin, Old Noakes, Gorhendad Oldbuck, the Proudfoots, and others. In Tolkien's lesser works this ebullience sometimes runs riot. *Farmer Giles of Ham* is rollicking, as is much of the early part of *The Hobbit*. The name Niggle in "Leaf by Niggle," not only holds up a mirror to this character but, since the story is in part autobiographical, a mirror also to the author's moderate view of himself. Fancy to the point of extravagance marks the accounts of Tom Bombadil's winning of Goldberry, of Tom's trip down the Withywindle and the hornpipe dance at old Maggot's house, of Little Princess Mee, of the Troll who munched on the shinbone of Tom's uncle Tim, of the Mewlips and the Oliphaunt and the fat cat on the mat dreaming of heroic deeds, of the great Fastitocalong, etc.

In the *Rings* this sense of humor is seldom immediately present yet frequently not far in the background. Indeed, I have heard serious readers insist that they thought Gandalf and Gollum humorous characters. If these are humorous then all are so except Sauron and the Ringwraiths. In the horrific danger of Cirith Ungol, Sam and Frodo disguise themselves in orc clothing. Sam looks Frodo over and says, "Well, there you are, Mr. Frodo. A perfect little orc." And even their conversation on the way up Orodruin, when they are suffering all but death itself, is not without a holy unction of humor. Of course Treebeard and Gimli and Legolas often delight with their joviality, and the group as a whole is in the fullest sense a "fellowship."

But of course sound in Tolkien is not confined to humorous names, images, or ideas. What we actually have is story growing out of the rich complex of a fine ear, a sense of humor, and philological acumen, and all conditioned by the larger power of imaginative conception. Tolkien's story arises from a footing of comparative linguistics, in which he is one of the world's best scholars. His names, for instance, do not normally appear from vacancy, a telephone book or "fancy" but from a matrix of Elvish and other invented languages. These in turn, while based upon structural principles, have as their models languages that Tolkien regards unusually beautiful. Of all the languages that stirred his young heart, Welsh was the greatest. "I heard it coming out of the west. It struck at me in the names on coal-trucks; and drawing nearer, it flickered past on station-signs, a flash of strange spelling and a hint of a language old and yet alive; even in an *adeiladwyd* 1887, ill-cut on a stone-slab, it pierced my linguistic heart. . . . It is the native language to which in unexplored desire we would still go home." [12]

Professor Tolkien tells also of being deeply stirred on first seeing a Gothic vocabulary, a bare list of words. Many readers of the *Rings* have the same experience in looking at the index of character names—Arwen, Balin, Baranor, Beren, Celeborn, Elbereth, Elendil, Elfstone, Entings, Gleowine, Lúthien, Mithrandir, Valandil—or of places— Beleriand, Celebrant, Dimholt, Dimrill Dale, Dwarrow-delf, Elvenhome, Helm's Deep, Ithilien, Númenor, Riven-dell, Tumladen, Westernesse, etc. Treebeard said that his Entish name was "like a story." Do not these names make imaginative voyagers of us all? And long-time lovers of the *Rings* find themselves in the same position as the group at Cormallen when the minstrel sang to them "until their hearts, wounded with sweet words, overflowed, and their joy was like swords, and they passed in thought out to regions where pain and delight flow together and tears are the very wine of blessedness." [13]

It is a fact that the subject matter and tone in Tolkien quite perfectly reflect the linguistic element. When thir-teen dwarves named Dwalin, Balin, Kili, Fili, Dori, Nori, Ori, Oin, Gloin, Bifur, Bofur, Bombur, and Thorin come bouncing into the quiet life of a sedentary hobbit, what can you expect of him except to be "confusticated," "flummoxed," and "bewuthered"? When on Page 1 Aegi-dius Ahenobarbus Julius Agricola de Hammo turns out to be simply Farmer Giles of Ham, we know immediately the general nature of the exploits he may engage in. In Norse myth Garm is a powerful dog guarding the gates of hell, but Tolkien with patent irony makes him in *Farmer Giles* a lazy dog more interested in his own skin than in guarding the farmer's house. If there is a subtle connec-tion of the name to "darn" and "charm" it is owing to that combination of feelings in the reader and could account for Tolkien's choice of the name. The delight of the "word-hoard" is as native to Tolkien as is paradox to G. K. Chesterton.

It is in the *Rings* that the phonological gift in Tolkien becomes exquisite and powerful. One admirer of this work said that the story ought to be sung rather than read. Once indeed when translating some Elvish for me he first began to read but then started over and sang the transla-tion. The *Rings* is a symphony in which a great number of

themes—heroic, joyous, cheerful, pensive, melancholic—
come together and whose tones are as varied and yet as
"chorded" as the languages of the Elves, the Orcs, and the
Ents:

ELVISH

A! Elbereth Gilthoniel!
silivren penna míriel
o menel aglar elenath!

ORKISH

Uglúk u bagronk sha pushdug
Saruman-glob búbhosh skai'.

ENTISH

Laurelindórian lindelorendor
malinornélion ornemalin.

and whose music enchants while it lifts the mind and
heart.

Why is the *Rings* being widely read today? At a time
when perhaps the world was never more in need of authentic experience, this story seems to provide a pattern of
it. A businessman in Oxford told me that when tired or
out of sorts he went to the *Rings* for restoration. Lewis
and various other critics believe that no book is more
relevant to the human situation. W. H. Auden says that it
"holds up the mirror to the only nature we know, our
own." [14] As for myself, I was rereading the *Rings* at the
time of Winston Churchill's funeral and I felt a distinct
parallel between the two. For a few hours the trivia which
normally absorbs us was suspended and people experi-
enced in common the meaning of leadership, greatness,
valor, time redolent of timelessness, and common trials.
Men became temporarily human and felt the life within
them and about. Their corporate life lived for a little and
made possible the sign of renewal after a realization such
as occurs only once or twice in a lifetime.

For a century at least the world has been increasingly
demythologized. But such a condition is apparently alien
to the real nature of men. Now comes a writer such as
John Ronald Reuel Tolkien and, as remythologizer,
strangely warms our souls.

Pieties and Giant Forms in
The Lord of the Rings

DANIEL HUGHES

No admirer of *The Lord of the Rings* needs to be told that Tolkien is to be taken seriously, but the range, the depth, the poetic risk of his accomplishment are, I think, insufficiently understood. The author's aesthetic, as expressed in his essay, "On Fairy-Stories," [1] written *after* the great trilogy was barely underway, can mislead us—unless we see it as an apologia and a program of work of the most ambitious kind. Tolkien allies himself with the Classical against the Romantic by describing the artistry of the fairy-story as "sub-creation;" but this perhaps unfortunate formulation does not imply that artistic activity is an inferior occupation or that "Fairy-Stories" constitute an inferior genre. By describing his work-to-be as sub-creation and the artist as a sub-creator, the author aligns himself with Shaftesbury's eighteenth-century notion of the artist as "a just Prometheus under Jove" rather than with Shelley's Tasso-oriented, *"Non merita nome di creatore, se non Iddio ed il Poeta."* But this by no means suggests that Tolkien does not take the artist or his creation with anything but complete seriousness. The Primary Creation is God's work, of course, but, in the making of "Faërie," which is *not* primarily for children, but for fallen adults, the artist (Tolkien has to be his own best uncited example) may actually assist in "the effoliation and multiple enrichment of creation." Part of his view is familiar enough: the artist is free to make what he wants, particularly in Fairy-Stories. ". . . in such 'fantasy,' as it is called, new form is made; Faërie begins; Man becomes a sub-creator." But note carefully how importantly Tolkien takes this secondary act:

> An essential power of Faërie is thus the power of making immediately effective by the will the visions of "fantasy." Not all are beautiful or even wholesome, not at any rate the fantasies of fallen Man. . . . This aspect of "mythology"—sub-creation rather than either representation or symbolic interpretation of the beauties and terrors of the world—is, I think, too little considered.

Although Tolkien is critical of Coleridge in his essay, surely the famous formulations of the *Biographia Literaria* have influenced him and can help us to appreciate what has been done in *The Lord of the Rings*. Coleridge writes of the imagination that, "this power, first put in action *by the will and understanding,* and retained under their irremissive, though gentle and unnoticed controul . . . reveals itself in the balance or reconciliation of opposite qualities." [2] The will, infected, but capable of redemption, *free to choose,* may float, may dream, but above all, must construct a conscious vision like the great fantasy-trilogy itself. Moreover, "Fantasy" is the particular goal and product of sub-creation which is superior to either "representation" or "symbolic interpretation." Fantasy in the form of "narrative art" thus becomes the purest mode of storytelling; in fact, the finest mode of literary art itself.

These are large claims, but it is important to understand what Tolkien is *not* doing. His sense of the term "fantasy" is not limited, he tells us, "to the queerness of things that have become trite, when they are suddenly seen from a new angle." This mode, exemplified by the preface to the *Lyrical Ballads,* cannot involve that full creative power which must make and create the *new.* Again, I think Coleridge can help us. *The Lord of the Rings* is a truly imaginative work in the Coleridgean sense as *The Once and Future King* by T. H. White, with which it is sometimes compared, is only a fanciful one, playing with "fixities and definites" that are plucked from a legend and history only half believed in. *The Hobbit* is itself, I think, a work of Fancy on its way to full imaginative confrontations. The trilogy of the Ring is constantly and organically growing as its remarkable narrative pace rushes the reader over hesitations into brilliant solutions of form and content. But what is this "new form" that Tolkien has made and made available to so many different kinds of readers and responders? How can a book so thoroughly conversant with the traditions yet refresh them? Answers to these questions bring us to the human heart of the great work.

The Lord of the Rings is a masterpiece which uses the forms of irony without an ironic effect. "Sub-creation," apart from its relevance to aesthetics, reminds us of the great Neo-Christian writer of our time, Simone Weil, whose grim and moving method of "de-creation" is ironical, too, a reduction from what we think we will be to what, in the divine perspective, we are. Thus, we should come to the Godhead as Shelley urges himself or his reader to join Adonais,

> then shrink
> Even to a point within our day and night;
> And keep thy heart light lest it make thee sink
> When hope has kindled hope, and lured thee to the brink.

Or shrink to a hobbit, for he is, essentially, a de-created human being, both better and less than ourselves. The hobbit is basically a tender parody of Vitruvian man, but seldom in his trilogy does Tolkien ever observe his grand concept as a *transplanted* figure in the manner of talking horse, wise fox, thoughtful pig; his conception maintains its integrity throughout in a context where the grandeur and dignity of being a hobbit, a reduced man, break constantly through. For the old forms themselves, saga, epic, fable, chronicle, romance, cannot shine directly for the modern reader. Tolkien restores these forms by putting the hobbit in the midst of them, in a mood where the creature is not overblown to carry an impossible burden nor Man lowered to meet him. The hobbit is the grand *donnée* of this fantasy, and we must understand how well he *works* before we can appreciate the unique and special quality of *The Lord of the Rings*.

We are told that only Gandalf among the Wise has gone in for hobbit-lore, "an obscure branch of knowledge, but full of surprises." Yet hobbits are neither mysterious nor magical. Their toughness, displayed unconvincingly by Bilbo in *The Hobbit*, but crucial in *The Rings*, is not the expression of super-powers. Harmlessness is the key to hobbit-essence; their height, between two and four feet; their hairy feet; their shyness; their would-be six meals a day; their feeling for a still-unfallen nature; their lack of interest in history and grand events—all these make them a moving dream of ourselves. Yet, except perhaps in the characterization of Frodo's squire, Sam Gamgee, Tolkien's avoidance of sentimentality is remarkable. He always keeps the hobbit in scale; once we accept the imaginative fact of hobbitry (and if we don't, why read the book at all?), the details of the long fiction follow in perfect order and with unquestionable imaginative coherence. Coleridge argued that in experiencing *The Tempest* the "principal and only genuine excitement ought to come from within—from the moved and sympathetic imagination." [3] In like manner should we follow the fortunes of the hobbit and his world; there is no other way to approach him. But neither the brilliantly managed conception of the hobbit nor the resources of a learning made new and executed to an astounding richness would bring the trilogy off as more than a don's obsessive winter dream were it not for the success Tolkien has with his hero and central character. In this day when only the antihero seems a viable protagonist in fiction and when the very idea of the hero must be diffused into the archetype and scattered in a thousand faces, the portrait of Frodo Baggins, the Ring-bearer, is a delicate triumph of art and attitude. Frodo, the nephew of Bilbo Baggins, the protagonist of *The Hobbit*, is the unlucky inheritor of the One Ring that must be given back, thrown into the Fire-Mountain in the heart of the evil land of Mordor. The Quest is his alone, and only he, Frodo of the peaceful Shire, can perform it.

Frodo is not an "interesting" character, conceived in the round or exhibiting a set of complicated and varied responses. He is that familiar figure at the center of the action, but, like David Copperfield, it is his goal and the events surrounding his purpose, not his character, that make him the center of attention. The charge that is laid on him is absurd; whereas Bilbo, his predecessor, went to find a treasure, Frodo goes forth to lose one. The consistent sense of renunciation in the central action of the trilogy heightens the elegiac tone that darkens especially the third volume, *The Return of the King*. But Frodo, though a hobbit and distinctly not an Elf or one of the Big Ones, is still, as Bilbo and Gandalf think him, the best hobbit in the Shire. He is intelligent, courageous, and true to his Quest, even as he is woefully and, it seems, overpoweringly, beset. Frodo's despair is illuminated, however, by Simone Weil's assertion that "we have all . . . impossible desires within us as a mark of our destination, and they are good for us when we no longer hope to accomplish them." [4] Hope is alleged to die frequently in this fiction, but such death is not merely a rhetorical device to deepen the next triumph; neither Frodo nor, I think, his creator understands, in the moment of despair, how hope can survive, but the true optimism of the work lies in its confident creative impulsion, always pushing to new solutions. Frodo's moment of decision at the Council of Elrond, when he agrees to take the Ring to Mordor, is not wholly his own; the historical moment of the Shire folk has come, "when they arise from their quiet fields to shake the towers and counsels of the great"; but he is fully responsible to his choice. There is never any sense that the dice of his ultimate success have been loaded.

Frodo's main temptation is to use the Ring to make himself invisible when his enemies pursue him, although he requires it less as his danger becomes greater, in Moria, in Shelob's Lair, in Mordor itself. But the gradual physical decline of Frodo stands in sharp contrast to the increased height and strength put on by Merry and Pippin, the hobbit-friends who initially accompany him on his Quest, but who, in the *ambiance* of Rohan and Gondor, "grow" and "change"—as Frodo does not; his wounds are too deep, his purpose too single. Despite the happy outcome of his Quest—the Ring is thrown into Mount Doom and the Dark Lord Sauron is defeated—he cannot stay in the Shire, but, with Gandalf and the elven king and queen, must take ship from the Grey Havens. To appreciate why Frodo's voyage out is so moving, even to the point of tragic tears, is to come closer to the human meaning of the hobbit image itself. Frodo does not die like the tragic hero, but he is nonetheless transported to another dimension where he can no longer truly be a hobbit. Frodo of the Shire is all our understanding of him, but the careful avoidance of the special, the magical, in that knowledge is overthrown by the hero's translation to exactly that realm Tolkien has presented so splendidly *apart* from, if *along with*, the hobbit in the fiction. Frodo's "death" is moving because the hobbit in ourselves must meet a new dispensation. Losing him, we are back in the mimetic world of fustian heroes on the one hand and fanciful Little People on the other, and not all the rich and complicated appendices in the world can soothe us for Frodo's suffering and departure. The mood is unmistakable: "Go, bid the soldiers shoot."

There are two other personages in *The Lord of the Rings* whose presence manifest almost as well as Frodo's the precision and delicately wrought poise of Tolkien's intentions: the dreadful Gollum, a parody of Frodo who yet performs a crucial act, and the wizard Gandalf, an essential mediating figure between the worlds of the fantasy. Gollum, the obsessed water-creature driven mad by his erstwhile possession of the Ring, as demonic as Frodo is an apocalyptic focus of energy, that loathsome being who, at the crucial moment, falls into Mount Doom with the Ring he has bitten from Frodo's finger—Gollum is one of the imaginative triumphs of the book. This figure is interesting in himself; his speech, "What has it got in its

pocketses," is the most memorable and immediately de-
tachable part of the book, but the "fun" one may have
with Gollum, so called for his gurgling throat, should not
obscure his larger meaning in the fiction. Gandalf predicts
that Gollum, whose initial recovery of the Ring is the key
plot device that brings hobbit and Ring together, will
have something to do before the end; and the fact is, of
course, that even Gollum is redeemed, in his extinction
saving what we have come to call the "civilized world."
Gandalf tells Frodo that Gollum's people were "of hob-
bit-kind," though surely of a downward-looking type!
When Sam Gamgee helps Frodo to trap Gollum in Book
Four, he is startled to find a resemblance between his
master and the grotesque creature; they are in some way
akin, and, of course, their kinship is their concern with the
Ring, Gollum to repossess it, Frodo to destroy it in the
manner decreed by the Council of Elrond. But they understand each other; the process by which Frodo comes to
pity Gollum, as Bilbo had before him, is an exact measure
of Frodo's mastery over himself as well as over the terrible
power of the Ring. Gollum, the anti-Frodo, completes our
picture of the book's courageous hero. Together, Frodo-
Gollum form one of the most convincing pictures of
obsession, how it is fought, how it is yielded to, in all
fiction.

The presence of the wizard Gandalf poses, I think, the
most difficult technical problem faced in the trilogy, one
not completely solved. The wizard, like the hobbit and
many of the other characters in the work, must be transformed to a greater strength and dignity—the passage from
Gandalf the Grey to Gandalf the White marking one
of the most important metamorphoses in *The Lord of the
Rings*. Gandalf begins in *The Hobbit*, and in the opening
pages of the later work, as a figure of Fancy, semicomical,
a bit fuddled as though his creator is somewhat uncertain
about what he should do with him. If Gandalf becomes
too competent, too able to control the action, too ready a
deus ex machina, his character will limit the imaginative
possibilities of hobbits and Men too much. In fact, Pip-

pin's cry at the siege of Gondor, "Gandalf, can't you do something?", must have been as frequent a temptation for the fabulist as it is a too-simple recourse for hobbit and reader. Gandalf is kept away from the plot for long stretches; he goes away in Book One, chapter four, not to return until Book Two, when, in a startling development, he disappears into the depths of Moria as he battles the monster Balrog; he then returns mysteriously in chapter five of Book Three, having undergone his great secret battle alone in the depths and on the mountain, for the rest of the work not only interpreter and guide, but a great Wizard Warrior, Gandalf the White, girded with the sword Glamdring and commanding his superb horse, Shadowfax. Yet the recognizable archetype of withdrawal and return cannot be used to explain the Gandalfian mystery. The extent of Gandalf's power remains unclear until the scene in Book Three, chapter ten, in which Gandalf confronts his alter ego, the fallen wizard, Saruman, once his superior, but now so hopelessly infected by the power of the Dark Lord that he seeks the One Ring for himself. Gandalf-Saruman is a pairing like Frodo-Gollum in which the lesser figure's lapse into madness helps to define the strengths, as well as the weaknesses, of the stronger. Like the hobbits, we have first admired Gandalf for his fireworks, the products of Fancy, but we have come to understand how deeply conceived a catalytic agent he really is in the fiction. Like Frodo, he finally sets sail from the Grey Havens because his role in historical time has ended, but it is good that he is on board; Frodo is not alone.

I have argued that the hobbit is neither mysterious nor magical; in fact, the central world of the novel, whether on the hobbit or heroic plane, maintains its own rational order and odd restraint. Yet the unpredictable reach of an imagination *not* balanced by form but extended beyond plot and narrative—an essential element in Tolkien's success—focuses on those figures who stand to one side of Frodo's Quest: Tom Bombadil, the Pan of Middle-earth; Treebeard, the Ent who embodies the spirit of trees; and, of course, the Elves who frame, but do not constrict, the deepest inner and outer worlds of *The Lord of the Rings*.

These characters point to a freedom the author cannot allow his main figures. We respond to them in their detachment, engendered as it is, I think, by the purity of motive exhibited in the creation of the hobbit himself. Simone Weil has argued that, "On God's part creation is not an act of self-expansion but of restraint and renunciation." [5] In literature, the artist (here, the fantasist, in Tolkien's term, the sub-creator) is God, and I insist, blasphemously perhaps, that the restraint and renunciation required of an author in choosing the lowly hobbit to bear the burden of his large narrative enables him to people his creation with the most convincing men and women of Faërie this critic has ever encountered. Tom Bombadil, who affects the action the least, is innocent, prelapsarian Nature, not a Noble Savage, but that timeless being, joyous in the woods, to whom the horrendous events of the Third Age of Middle-earth can have little meaning. He is even impervious to the power of the Ring, for, when Frodo puts it on, Tom can still see him. At the same time, as Gandalf warns, Tom Bombadil stands outside the cataclysmic events of the Third Age and cannot be called upon for help; he has withdrawn to his own limits and will not come forward until there is "a change of days." But Treebeard, the Ent, a kind of Tree-Man — slow-moving, thoughtful, immemorial — unlike Bombadil, does participate in the wars against Sauron; Merry and Pippin inspire him to call the Entmoot at which the decision is made to march on and destroy Isengard, Saruman's retreat. The Ent is one of Tolkien's happiest inventions, an image reminiscent of Hopkins and Wordsworth in those poems of fierce attachment to a natural world whose inscapes are threatened with destruction. Pathos too surrounds Treebeard because the Entwives have been missing for many years so there can be no Entings. How long, Tolkien asks in Bombadil and Treebeard, can nature, which we so mishandle, survive as pure natural song or leaf?

The Elves are the very presence of grace in *The Lord of the Rings,* the boundary of imaginative possibility; they must be taken with complete seriousness, but in a different tonality than the hobbits themselves. Nostalgia and remorse surround their natures because they have been moving west out of the Grey Havens for many years: an intimation that we, as men, are seeing them for the last time that contributes strongly to the subtle sense of loss as the book both darkens and lightens its meanings. In "Of Fairy-Stories," Tolkien speaks of "a kind of elvish craft" by which the Secondary World built up in Fantasy will engender Secondary Belief in its existence, so we must assume that he believes in Elves as he believes in hobbits. One of the Elves, Legolas, becomes part of the Fellowship of the Ring, and his soothing and superior presence on the journey from Rivendell, his stamina and bowmanship, his courtly and lyrical manner strengthen and dignify the Quest, even as they set him apart from the others. But it is the two great chapters of Book Two, "Lothlórien" and "The Mirror of Galadriel," that best exhibit the role of the Elves in the trilogy. Lórien is an Earthly Paradise where the Elves bide their time, ruled by the elven-king Celeborn and his lady Galadriel. Tolkien is precise in his arrangement: in Rivendell, where the Council of Elrond takes place, there is a *memory* of ancient things, but in Lórien, the doomed elven world of the present, the ancient things live on in the waking world. There is no stain in Lórien, it is true, but even here, in its most perfect setting, the work's note of pathos, of loss can be heard. If Frodo fails, Lórien will be at the mercy of Sauron the Dark Lord; but, even if he succeeds, the power of Lórien will be diminished because such triumph will signify the end of the Third Age when the Elves must depart for the West and the Grey Havens—as they do. But the Elves are not basically presences of sorrow. They offer the strongest joy the imagination can bring, beyond and above our world. Early on, as Frodo, Pippin, and Merry start their marvellous journey, the true elven note is struck, never to be forgotten by the wanderers; the reader tunes his ears:

> Away high in the East swung Remmirath, the Netted Stars, and slowly above the mists red Borgil rose, glowing

like a jewel of fire. Then by some shift of airs all the mist was drawn away like a veil, and there leaned up, as he climbed over the rim of the world, the Swordsman of the Sky, Menelvagor with his shining belt. The Elves all burst into song. (Bk. I, chap. 3)

I have yet to examine what for many readers may be the most striking feat of *The Lord of the Rings*: its resuscitation of the Heroic Age, its virtues and valors intact. Most of us read Homer today, probably in Richmond Lattimore's fine translation, without much insight or interest in the heroic and epic materials in themselves. Tolkien, in writing for *now*, even through his removed world, has succeeded in doing what might have been thought impossible in our ostensibly liberal-democratic, war-hating times; he has almost brought off an epic as grand as *Beowulf*, as detailed as an old dim chronicle, and as old-fashioned in its values as an Icelandic saga or Sir Walter Scott. The internal creative process of the book, as organic as any Coleridgean plant, comes to flower nowhere more dynamically than in the presentation of the wars of the Ring, whether Tolkien is relating the stately muster of Rohan or the startling account of the siege of Gondor. But these could not come to pass, I think, without the swelling, growing role of Aragorn, whose passage from anonymous Ranger (called Strider) to the grand restored king of Gondor and the fulfilment of the line of the Númenoreans is the central event of the "external" and "historical" part of the work as the Quest of Frodo is crucial to its "private" and "personal" side. In his introductory note to the reprinting of "On Fairy-Stories" Tolkien admits that when he and the hobbits got to Bree (Bk. I, chap. 2), he had no idea who Strider was, that cloaked and possibly sinister figure who is very curious about the hobbits and their appearance in a hostelry so far from the Shire. It is exactly here, I submit, when the author discovers who Strider is and what he wants to do with him that *The Lord of the Rings* starts to assume its large but never baggy shape. Strider is the image that enables Tolkien, the artist, fantasist, and theorist of Faërie, to join hands with

Tolkien the admirer of the Heroic Age's tales and devices. The extraordinary excitement surrounding the figure of Aragorn as it develops almost tilts the balance of the book, nearly takes it too far from the hobbit, especially in the later scenes in Gondor. But the mediating presence of Gandalf and the roles of the minor hobbits, Merry with the Riders of Rohan, Pippin with the beseiged men of Gondor, keep the imaginative proportions in place, though certainly we have moved very far from that erstwhile children's book that launched the whole creative enterprise.

With the breaking of the fellowship that closes Book Two, the remaining four books of the trilogy divide precisely into two parts, Books Three and Five belonging to the Heroic Age, Books Four and Six to the theme of the Quest, with the middle pages of Six bringing the two parts together again when the Eagles sent by Gandalf rescue Frodo and Sam from exploding Mount Doom. (The last three chapters, modelled on the return of Odysseus, extend the book more than is necessary perhaps; we know the Third Age is coming to an end and sense Frodo will have to depart before he actually goes). The communal splendor of Books Three and Five is carefully placed against the agonizing progress of Frodo to Mordor in Four and Six, although there is never a sense that the book has split in two because we never forget that Frodo's approach is made grander by the gathering armies in the background. It's interesting to note that Tolkien tells us that he wrote Book Three and part of Book Five before he began Book Four, as though delaying to gird himself for his hero's worst moment; indeed, Book Four, with the wounding and apparent death of Frodo marks the lowest descent of the author's vision. But the successful campaign against Saruman in Book Three and the breaking of the Siege of Gondor in Book Five hint at the possible incredible resolution of Frodo's mission. The hobbits have their place indeed in the grand events of these days. The heinous Captain of the Ringwraiths is slain by the lady Éowyn and the hobbit Merry when, in avenging their fallen King Théoden, the hobbit, who has not had much status in the work, stabs his enemy from behind, thus bringing together heroic confrontation and hobbit guile. The death of this dreadful creature demonstrates the true nature of the demons in Tolkien's world; his hauberk and mantle become immediately empty and his cry, bodiless and thin, "was never heard again in that age of this world." And Meriadoc Brandybuck takes his place among the great warriors of the ages.

There is some truth in the complaint voiced by a few critics that the Opposition in *The Lord of the Rings* is too simply conceived. As a Christian optimist Tolkien believes in heroism and the rise of the lowly, but his Orcs, the general troops of evil in the book, are creepy-crawly figures more akin to the sadistic small horrors glimpsed in the corner of Fra Angelico than they are to the powerful, embodied visions of Dante. But the larger set pieces of demonic confrontation in the book—the Balrog who disappears with Gandalf into Moria, the noisome Shelob who terrorizes Sam and Frodo in the tunnel leading to Mordor—these are impressive figures of nightmare. Like Blake, whose engravings present few visually impressive images of the demonic, Tolkien would not dwell on the beasties themselves, but on the mental strife of the would-be Christians who are trying to wake from Error. His finest decision in this regard is surely his keeping Sauron, the Dark Lord of the Rings, off the center of his stage except as a powerful Roving Eye whose presence is felt everywhere but whose direct specific embodiment is not required. Besides, we get our direct encounter with Evil in Saruman's Tower of Orthanc in Book Three; a frontal attack on Barad-dûr, Sauron's tower, could be only repetitious. Indeed, Saruman is like Blake's Urizen because Isengard under his direction has become a place of heartless machines and wheels. Just as Urizen yields to the less concrete but more terrible figure of Satan in the prophetic Books, so Saruman, a figure unable to contain the deeper disorder required for the full working out of the drama of the Quest, must be replaced by Sauron whose *essence* must be dealt with in the apocalyptic moment of the Third Age of Middle-earth. The Heroic Age does not require rounded villains—Tolkien has the tradition too firmly in hand to require them; and the Quest theme is, as I have said, a renunciation, a surrender. Noble villains not needed.

The energy displayed in all these matters, the hobbit and the Heroic Age, the Quest and its Nightmares, comes to no more splendid expression than in the best poem of the many in the work, a successful recreation of Anglo-Saxon verse in its own right, but in its context, following the death of Théoden, King of Rohan, while Frodo somewhere, somehow struggles toward Mount Doom, an overpoweringly moving and splendid moment. The shining piety and the deep imaginative strength of the book flash forth from the full orchestra.

> *We heard of the horns in the hills ringing,*
> *the swords shining in the South-kingdom.*
> *Steeds went striding to the Stoningland*
> *as wind in the morning. War was kindled.*
> *There Théoden fell, Thengling mighty,*
> *to his golden halls and green pastures*
> *in the Northern fields never returning,*
> *high lord of the host. Harding and Guthláf,*
> *Dúnhere and Déorwine, doughty Grimbold,*
> *Herefara and Herubrand, Horn and Fastred,*
> *fought and fell there in a far country:*
> *in the Mounds of Mundburg under mould they lie*
> *with their league-fellows, lords of Gondor.*
> *Neither Hirluin the Fair to the hills by the sea,*
> *nor Forlong the old to the flowering vales*
> *ever, to Arnach, to his own country*
> *returned in triumph; nor the tall bowmen,*
> *Derufin and Duilin, to their dark waters,*
> *meres of Morthond under mountain-shadows.*
> *Death in the morning and at day's ending*
> *lords took and lowly. Long now they sleep*
> *under grass in Gondor by the Great River.*
> *Grey now as tears, gleaming silver,*
> *red then it rolled, roaring water:*
> *foam dyed with blood flamed at sunset;*

as beacons mountains burned at evening;
red fell the dew in Rammas Echor.

Though *The Lord of the Rings* is predicated on classical assumptions, and a classical aesthetic, it reminds us
more of Romantic poetry—of Blake in its search for restored methods and images; of Wordsworth in its pieties
and tones. When Blake writes jauntily in the preface to
Jerusalem that he is again "displaying his Giant forms to
the public," we smile, knowing how small an audience he
had and understanding that his forms are only now finding their public through collective labors nearly equal to
the intensity of the forms themselves. I am not suggesting
that the popular *Lord of the Rings* is equal in density or
subtlety to the Prophetic Books, but it moves in that
direction by refusing to be allegory, or representational in
the low mimetic sense of that term. Like Blake, Tolkien
distrusts allegory because he seeks the detached experience
of what he calls "sub-creation" which we, in seeking to
purge the term of any false connotations, may better
understand by Geoffrey H. Hartman's "Pure Representation" in which "the poet represents the mind as knowing
without a cause from perception." [6] We cannot perceive a
hobbit, but we can imagine one, *without* resemblances or
assemblings from the known world. Attempts to allegorize
the trilogy from the First or Second World Wars can only
limit, even demean, what has been accomplished. Of
course, as Tolkien admits, the loss of his friends in the
first war might have had something to do with his personal feelings in his book, and I think the threat of
Nazism is somewhere in its propulsive stirrings. But—horrors!—Sauron is not Hitler nor Frodo Winston Churchill.
The giant forms of Tolkien's world, however, do not show
the psychic and archetypal energies of Blake's creations;
they are—we have known it all the time—the great modes
and methods of English literature itself which here, indi-
rectly, finds one of its finest tributes. The trilogy is a
triumph and riot of a deep traditional learning well lived
and well wrought.

Tolkien's tone is not very Blakean; it is basically pious,

pious of English letters and the English countryside, pious
in its observation of man's place in a hostile world where
he must make his way. Somewhere between Dickens and
Wordsworth, particularly the latter, *The Lord of the
Rings* finds its refreshened tonalities. The Heroic Age,
"Milton, thou shouldst be living at this hour!" and the
private Quest (compare the "unfathered vapour" of Imagination in *The Prelude*) come together in what Wordsworth hoped would be a poetry of healing and "recom-
pense." So in Tolkien joy may live and new forms arise.
"On Fairy-Stories" concludes:

> All tales may come true; and yet, at the last, redeemed,
> they may be as like and as unlike the forms that we give
> them as Man, finally redeemed, will be like and unlike the
> fallen that we know.

Tolkien's Fantasy
The Phenomenology of Hope

GUNNAR URANG

For J. R. R. Tolkien fantasy is the art of creating an "other world." It is an "elvish craft," and the "secondary world" thus produced is a realm of enchantment.[1] As a multitude of readers can now testify, to enter the "other world" called Middle-earth is to encounter both the strange and the familiar and, emanating from them, an extraordinary power. My purpose here is to consider the manifestations of that imaginative power, moving from its other-worldly aspects toward that within it which lies closer to home.

To one who is reading *The Lord of the Rings*[2] for the first time, that power may be felt simply as a *sense* of depths, of rich implications in the work. But depth and richness, considered analytically, become levels or dimensions; and I shall try to suggest, in brief, the three dimensions of *The Lord of the Rings*. On reading Tolkien's work we find ourselves first in a dimension of *wonder*, the effect of authentic fantasy. On further reading and rumination, we sense also a dimension of *import* or meaningfulness, the allegorical thrust of the fantasy. Finally, we may discover a dimension of incipient *belief*, which is a function of the "rhetoric" of this fiction, of what I have dared to call its "strategy."

First of all, then, the appeal of *The Lord of the Rings* lies in the fact that it *is*—so wholeheartedly and unabashedly—fantasy. This is the realm of Faërie, where dwell elves, fays, witches, trolls, and dragons; where sky and sea, tree and stone, bird and beast can all be changed by magical enchantment; and where men, too, can see strange sights and be made capable of more-than-human deeds. The literary expression of what is conceived by the fantastic imagination carries a quality of strangeness and wonder. It awakes in the reader an equivalent sense of wonder, as well as a longing for this other mode of life. In fact, Tolkien insists, fantasy of this sort contributes to the satisfaction of certain primordial human desires; and to be successful it need not convince the reader of the possibility, but only of the desirability, of the Secondary World.[3]

I am not arguing that Tolkien is correct in granting fantasy such universal powers. But I do find that his own conviction about it stands him in good stead. It inspires him to invent not a "thin," sketchy other-world as a mere frame for allegory but a rich, substantial world. It carries him so far, indeed, that to the one-thousand-plus pages of narrative he appends (in smaller type) over one hundred pages of miscellaneous information about Middle-earth. It also gives him the boldness to plunge us directly and totally into the fantasy realm, rather than to take us there from the earth we know by spaceship or time machine, or to bring the powers of another, occult world into everyday human life.

The events of the story take place at a time and in a place which are for us indeterminate, but which are identified in the book as the Third Age of Middle-earth. Any member in good standing of the Tolkien Society of America could give us a wealth of data about the topographical features of this region and its climatic conditions. What is important for us, however, is not where the forest and mountains of Middle-earth *are*, but what special sort of menace a forest or a mountain can be. For everything in this fantasy-world is thus capable of being more "alive," more "personal," so to speak, than its counterpart in our everyday world.

A number of the creatures living in this environment are also other than ordinary. In places like Mirkwood or Lothlórien one sees the fair, tall forms of Elves and hears their lovely singing. There are unimaginably evil creatures, too, such as the Balrog, who drove the Dwarves out of the mines of Moria under the Misty Mountains, or the spider-like monster Shelob, who lurks in a tunnel near one of the entrances to the land of Mordor. The Ents, perhaps Tolkien's most successful invention, are giant tree-shepherds, both man-like and tree-ish, and appropriately deliberate in speech and action. The Free Peoples of Middle-earth face also the total and persistent enmity of Sauron, the Dark Lord, who dwells in desolate, mountain-walled Mordor. He does his destructive work through the animalistic counterfeits of elves called Orcs and through the faceless, black-robed Ringwraiths. Sauron is opposed most effectively by Gandalf the Grey, one of the Wizards who came to Middle-earth earlier in the Third Age as "messengers sent to contest the power of Sauron, and to unite all those who had the will to resist him" (III, 365).

Gandalf works primarily with Men, since Middle-earth is becoming more and more *their* world—especially with the men of Gondor in the South, in whom is the blood of the ancient heroic Númenoreans from across the Sea. He also has much to do with certain hobbits. These are another Tolkien invention, the most important one for the fantasy, since they "carry" the burden of the story. The hobbits are a little people (their height ranging from two to four feet), with hair-covered and tough-soled feet, so that they seldom wear shoes. They are farmers and craftsmen, with little love for complicated machines. The good life, in their view, consists largely in eating and drinking (six meals a day when they can get them), in pipe-smoking (which they invented), and in giving or going to parties. The several varieties of hobbits live together quite amicably, in a little-known region called the Shire, with a minimum of government and having as little as possible to do with the world "outside."

It is through the experiences and impressions of the four hobbits who undertake the Quest and leave the safety of the Shire that we as readers learn the geography and ethnography of Middle-earth. Through them also we absorb a sense of its past. Nothing—short of actually reading the story—can begin to convey the richness of the historical context Tolkien has created for his "world." The inhabitants of Middle-earth, C. S. Lewis says, "are at once stricken and upheld by the memory of vanished civilizations and lost splendour." [4] Those memories become particularly poignant as the Third Age draws toward its crisis, toward the same sort of decisive struggle with the Dark Power which has marked the end of the other two ages.

That decisive struggle provides the context for the fantastic *events* that take place in the fantasy-*world* I have attempted, briefly, to describe. The pattern is that of the traditional Quest. It develops in the three stages which Northrop Frye has noted as characteristic: (1) the perilous journey and the concomitant preliminary adventures, (2) the crucial struggle, (3) the exaltation of the hero. [5] This perilous journey is undertaken, however, not to find a treasure but to get rid of one. A hobbit named Frodo Baggins has come into the possession of a magic ring which makes its wearer vanish. It is the greatest of the Rings of Power, the one into which Sauron let a great part of his power pass. Frodo's mission is to put this Ring beyond the grasp of the Enemy forever. He is given the aid of his neighbor Sam Gamgee, two other hobbit friends, Merry and Pippin, and five other representatives of the Free Peoples, the nine of them making up the Fellowship of the Ring. Some of them become involved in open war against Sauron's forces. The crucial struggle, however, is Frodo's and Sam's ordeal in bearing the Ring to Mount Doom in Mordor. When the heart of the mountain at last receives the Ring which was forged within its fiery depths, the Dark Tower is demolished and the power of Sauron broken.

What lifts this story, however, above mere "popular" fantasy fiction, what elicits a response beyond simple excitement and closer to authentic wonder is a certain tone and a certain aura of significance which are felt to surround the fantastic figures and their adventures. Northrop

Frye and his disciples have taught us to account for much of this sense of import by identifying these figures as archetypal and the story as mythic. And it is clear that Tolkien does take much of his material from sources close to their roots in ritual and myth. We can detect archetypal resonance in certain images which take on a function reminiscent of motifs in primitive religions—the power emanating from the Ringwraiths, for example, or the healing touch of Aragorn the king, or the sense of the numinous about the wizard Gandalf:

> His hair was white as snow in the sunshine; and gleaming white was his robe; the eyes under his deep brows were bright, piercing as the rays of the sun; power was in his hand. Between wonder, joy, and fear they stood and found no words to say. (II, 98)

But the modern reader's imagination cannot be said to respond to the exploits of a Gandalf in precisely the way a more primitive mind would respond to the mythological stories of the tribe's savior-king. This is not canonical myth but mythopoeic literature; that is, the author has created a story which speaks with something of the authority of the old myths. But only with something analogous to that authority. Tolkien, I am saying, does not "believe in" Gandalf so much as he believes in something that Gandalf represents. Ultimately the "seriousness" of "serious" fantasy lies not in the fantastic symbols as such but in the conceptions to which they—however ambiguously—refer. Which implies, I maintain, that our response to literary myth will be to some degree that which is appropriate to the allegorical mode. Tolkien himself speaks of the fairy-story (or fantasy) as having three faces: "the Mystical towards the Supernatural; the Magical towards Nature; and the Mirror of scorn and pity towards Man. The essential face of Faërie is the middle one, the Magical. But the degree in which the others appear (if at all) is variable, and may be decided by the individual storyteller." [6]

Read allegorically, *The Lord of the Rings* has much to

say about power, particularly a kind of power the use of which is inherently evil. For the Ring symbolizes, I think, power over the wills and destinies of other creatures; it is, we are told, the "One Ring to rule them all." To seek such power is to usurp a right that even God himself relinquishes, that of over-riding freedom; therefore the Ring is presented as inherently evil, not merely capable of being *mis*-used. The one who does use the Ring, instead of being the possessor of its power, becomes possessed by the power that made it. There is only one thing to do: repudiate that kind of power, absolutely. The Ring must go back to the primordial fire. The Quest itself, then, if I may condense the rich implications of the story even more drastically, is an allegory of heroism. As William Blissett argues, we find here a technique of composite characterization; Frodo and his company (which includes Gandalf the wizard; Aragorn, the rightful king of the West; a Man, from Gondor, named Boromir; Legolas the Elf; and a Dwarf named Gimli; as well as the other three hobbits) comprise the complete hero.[7]

But the significance of *The Lord of the Rings* is to be found not primarily in the dialectical alignment of its figures and forces but in the dynamic pattern of its action. Our critical concern must be not only with *what* we come to know but with *how* we come to know it; we ask not just what the Quest is about but whether it can succeed. This brings us, first of all, to questions of narrative technique. Basically, the "point of view," as I have suggested, is that of the four hobbits. We are meant to see things their way —as the ordinary coming to know the heroic, the everyday encountering the supernatural, the uninvolved becoming committed, and the weak and fearful wondering about their chances. But this point of view is not a closely restricted one. Tolkien offers a good indirect explanation of his method by way of a conversation between Frodo and Sam about tales of adventure. One of the subjects is happy endings. Sam notes that not all the people in tales go on to a good end—but then he adds a distinction: "at least not to what folk inside a story and not outside it call a good end" (II, 321). We, as readers, I am suggesting, are "inside" the story with Frodo and Sam and the others; but we are also "outside," inasmuch as Tolkien always makes sure that we know more, at any point, than any character in the story does. "Inside" or "outside" the story, the main question is whether or not a happy ending is possible; allegorically, whether or not there are, in the battle against evil, any grounds for *hope*.

Those "inside" the story hear many exhortations to hope and receive or discover such tokens as the crystal phial which Frodo is given by the Lady Galadriel of Lothlórien (it contains light from Eärendil, the star of hope). To note just one illustrative passage, Sam, in the desolation of Mordor, also finds hope in a star:

> Far above the Ephel Dúath in the West the night-sky was still dim and pale. There, peeping among the cloud-wrack above a dark tor high up in the mountains, Sam saw a white star twinkle for a while. The beauty of it smote his heart, as he looked up out of the forsaken land, and hope returned to him. For like a shaft, clear and cold, the thought pierced him that in the end the Shadow was only a small and passing thing: there was light and high beauty for ever beyond its reach. (III, 199)

"Inside" the tale, with Frodo or Sam, the reader feels their anxiety about the outcome, sees signs, and hears exhortations and reproofs. But from his higher point of vantage he discerns hopeful *patterns* as well. Now, it must be understood at this point that the reader is to receive Tolkien's work, imaginatively, as a kind of analogy-to-history. The reference in the Foreword to "sources" such as the "Red Book of Westmarch" and the "Book of the Kings" of Gondor, the supplementary chronicles and genealogies in the various appendices, and many other comparable devices strengthen this impression. The patterning I have alluded to constitutes, then, something like a theology—not a philosophy, but a theology—of history.

First, there is clearly a "providential" design, a sense of the interrelatedness of all the elements in this "history" and of an ordering of all these elements to one end. It is at the climactic moment of the Quest that both the interrelatedness and the ordering are felt most intensely. Here Tolkien points most sharply the paradox of providence and freedom, the conviction that "God creates freedom and yet dares to preordain the consummation." [8] Frodo and Sam are on Mount Doom; the others of the Company stand in peril outside the Black Gate of Mordor. Their fate depends upon what Frodo does next. Yet Frodo would not have reached the mountain had it not been for their diversionary maneuver. They in turn would not be occupying the attention of the great red eye of Sauron except for the fact that, much earlier, there had been a breakup of the Fellowship. That separation came as a result, however, of Boromir's free and self-willed act. What Frodo does at the moment of crisis is, of course, equally free and self-willed. "I have come," he cries out. "But I do not choose now to do what I came to do. I will not do this deed. The Ring is mine!" And he sets it on his finger and vanishes. But the Ring-obsessed hobbit-like creature called Sméagol, or Gollum, is also there, having followed them (and even, for a time, led them) into Mordor. So that finally it is the utterly lost Gollum who brings the reign of Sauron to an end. He rushes forward, wrestles madly with the unseen hobbit, bites off Frodo's ring finger, loses his balance, and falls wailing "Precious" into the abyss (III, 223–24). "Let us remember," Gandalf had said earlier, "that a traitor may betray himself and do good that he does not intend" (III, 89).

For both those "inside" and those "outside" the story, then, glimpses and prophetic revelations of this providential design yield hope for the outcome. But *The Lord of the Rings*, as "history," is more than day-to-day, on-going history. It is the history of the *end*; it is eschatology. And despite Tolkien's many other debts to "Northernness," the shape of this eschatology is not that of Norse mythology but that of the Christian tradition. Tolkien's myth of the end is no Ragnarök; the twilight is not for any gods but for Sauron and his forces.

What the hobbits have become enmeshed in is a decisive struggle of cosmic scope. This is, of course, the imagery of biblical eschatology; the end is not an apex, but a crisis. It is a time of intense suffering for the faithful, who often lose hope. The chief instrument of their torment is —in the mythological language of the Christian Apocalypse—a kind of "Antichrist," which the biblical scholar H. H. Rowley characterizes as "an individualizing of opposition in the figure of a monster of iniquity, who will treacherously attack his weak and unsuspecting neighbors, but who will be smitten and destroyed by God in a resounding disaster." [9]

The "resounding disaster" which overtakes Sauron is the work of a kind of composite hero: Gandalf, Aragorn, and Frodo. For the hobbits, the series of "epiphanies" of Aragorn as promised king are signs of hope; and his coronation, the fulfillment of that hope, is narrated with descriptive imagery that recalls some of the messianic portions of the Old Testament. Even more significant as a basis for hope is the pattern of happenings which we (and to some extent they) see developing, a series of unexpected rescues, of lesser "happy endings" figuring forth the ultimate triumph. The list is a long one: Old Forest, the River Bruinen, Mount Caradhras, Fangorn, Helm's Deep, the gates of Minas Tirith, the Pelennor Fields, Cirith Ungol, the Black Gate of Mordor, Mount Doom. In every one of these, despair is abruptly transformed to joy by a sudden and unexpected display of (often magical) power. The agent in most of these is Gandalf, and the supreme display of his powers is his return from the dead, after the fall into the abyss at Moria. This becomes the sign of signs, the profoundest basis for hope. Pippin, close to despondency in Minas Tirith, expresses it very simply: "No, my heart will not yet despair. Gandalf fell and has returned and is with us" (III, 39).

[Tolkien's fantasy speaks of the nature of the struggle against evil, the inescapability of involvement, the qualities of heroism, and the possibilities of real loss in that encounter. It also declares the viability of hope.] The happy ending is meant to be taken very seriously. In his essay "On Fairy-Stories," Tolkien theologizes the happy ending, for which he invents the term *eucatastrophe.* That "sudden, joyous 'turn,' " he says, gives a fleeting glimpse of a Joy which goes beyond the sense of wonder aroused by effective fantasy. It is analogous to the believer's joy in the birth of Christ, which is the eucatastrophe of man's history, or in the Resurrection, the eucatastrophe of the story of the Incarnation. "It may be," says Tolkien, "a far-off gleam or echo of *evangelium* in the real world." [10]

But, someone protests at this point, there is in *The Lord of the Rings* neither religious ritual nor belief in God. Aside from a few enigmatic hints, this is true. Only the *patterns* of providential ordering and eschatological crisis are there. I find in this work something like what Tolkien, in his famous Gollancz Memorial Lecture of 1936, claimed to see in *Beowulf.* He points out in the lecture that in the poem as we have it we can see signs that a "conversion" of the old materials had been taking place. Differences between Beowulf and Hrothgar, for instance, indicate that the narrator knew both the newer Christian poetry and the older heroic verse and could contemplate the new faith and learning and the native tradition together. Tolkien suggests that the author, having such a historical perspective, tended to *suppress* both the old gods and the specifically Christian references. "The language of *Beowulf,*" he concludes, "is in fact partly 're-paganized' by the author with a special purpose." [11]

It appears that *The Lord of the Rings* has also been partly "re-paganized" by its author with a special purpose. That "purpose" is related to what might be called an apologetic "strategy." Tolkien is at once committed to certain insights of traditional Christian belief and aware of the modern man's skepticism about many of those insights. Therefore, "re-paganization." After all, as Tolkien's friend the late C. S. Lewis once put it, "paganism is the religion of poetry, through which the author can express, at any moment, just so much or so little of his real religion as his art requires." [12]

The Lord of the Rings, then, although it presents no "God," no "Christ," and no "Christians," embodies much of Tolkien's "real religion" and is a profoundly Christian work. No "God" is required in this story; it is enough if it suggests the kind of pattern in history which the Christian tradition has ascribed to the providence of God. Gandalf and Aragorn need not turn our thoughts to the Christ of Christian faith; but they persuade us that if we are to have hope in our lives and in our history it must be hope *for* the kind of power and authority revealed in Aragorn the king and *on the basis of* the kind of power revealed in Gandalf's "miracles" and in his rising from the dead. What Frodo does and undergoes speaks to us of what a man's responsibility, according to the Christian faith, must always be: to renounce the kind of power which would enslave others and ourselves and to submit to that power which frees us to be all we are capable of being.

As for the theme of hope—Tolkien is content to work out something like a "phenomenology of hope." By analogy, through the images of fantasy, he suggests its "structure" in our experience, hope as it "appears" to us, with other concerns—metaphysical and theological—"bracketed." What is it like to face the approaching end of all things and yet experience hope? In this paper I have stressed two points in the answer rendered by Tolkien's fantasy. I have said that this experience presupposes an ordering of the historical process to some end and that it comes to be based on "signs" and paradigm-events within that history. Tolkien has created an imaginative framework—nothing more explicit than that—for the Christian experience of hope.

Needless to say, this theory about "apologetic strategy" has not satisfied my protest-ant reader. He is still shaking his head and saying, "That is not what *The Lord of the Rings* is; that is not it, at all." To answer him I should have to speak of Tolkien's fantasy not as allegory, but—as Tolkien did of *Beowulf,* in 1936—as *mythical* allegory. For one thing, to say that this work is myth rather than mere allegory is to take note of the fact that it contains a good deal of "unassigned" imagery, in contrast to the one-to-one correspondence between symbol and concept toward which allegory tends. As C. S. Lewis has said, the primary appeal of myth is to the imagination; its "indirect and further appeal to the will and the understanding can therefore be diversely interpreted according as the reader is a Christian, a politician, a psychoanalyst, or what not." [13] There are intimations of significance, all right. But "a myth points, for each reader, to the realm he lives in most. It is a master key; use it on what door you like." [14]

There is another sense, too, in which one may want to say that Tolkien has created literary myth. This has to do not with the quality of the imagery in the work but with the quality of the *imagination* that created it. In his lecture on *Beowulf*, Tolkien, unknowingly and beforehand, was arguing the case of his own fiction. "Myth," he said then, means "becoming largely significant—as a whole, accepted unanalyzed." And "it is at its best when it is presented by a poet who feels rather than makes explicit what his theme portends; who presents it incarnate in the world of history and geography. . . . For myth is alive at once and in all its parts, and dies before it can be dissected." [15] Tolkien has done precisely this: presented "what his theme portends" "incarnate in the world of history and geography." What we are conscious of first in *The Lord of the Rings* is also, I think, what will linger longest in memory: a new world, its geography and history, its inhabitants, its mysteries. The names he has borrowed and invented, the different speech styles, the imagery, and the rhythms create a realm in which there is traffic between the natural and the human, between the present and primordial times, between symbol and concept, just as there tends to be in the primitive myth-making imagination. We listen to Pippin trying to describe what it was like to look into the eyes of Treebeard the Ent:

> One felt as if there was an enormous well behind them, filled up with ages of memory and long, slow, steady thinking; but their surface was sparkling with the present:

like sun shimmering on the outer leaves of a vast tree, or on the ripples of a very deep lake. I don't know, but it felt as if something that grew in the ground—asleep, you might say, or just feeling itself as something between root-tip and leaf-tip, between deep earth and sky had suddenly waked up, and was considering you with the same slow care that it had given to its own inside affairs for endless years. (II, 66–67)

At such a movement the reader does not ask whether Tolkien "believes in" this creature of his imagination or in some concept which it stands for. The question of belief becomes, momentarily, irrelevant.

But irrelevant only for a moment and only because meaning and belief are *included* in the reception of the vivid image which has been presented to the imagination. That image continues to tease us also with intimations of import, so that we begin to entertain various possibilities of meaning. I have tried to sketch the shape of the thematic pattern which emerges, not in such a way, I hope, as to "dissect" the myth and thus do it to death but in such a way as to enrich our appreciation of its complex life. To see *The Lord of the Rings* only as an allegory of Christian hope is to see it for *less*—much less—than what it is. Not to see it thus at all is to see it for something *other* than what it is.

And it is also to miss much of its contemporary relevance. Our times have seen huge, destructive concentrations of economic power. Totalitarian regimes have come near to controlling not only the outward circumstances but the very wills of their people. In more subtle and more socially accepted ways men have used the powers of the mass media to manipulate human desires. Always in the back of our mind lurk the nightmare images of hydrogen bomb devastation. And still we see leaders—"ours" as well as "theirs"—standing, as it were, upon the very Crack of Doom and preparing to put on the Ring. It is not surprising that "the peculiar problem of our own day," as the English philosopher of religion Langmead Casserley declares, "is the widespread death of hope, a prevalent feeling that the end of all things is indeed at hand, unrelieved by any faith that this at the same time means that the Kingdom of God is near." [16] The gross mis-use in our time of immensely augmented powers is simply a fact. The widespread death of hope is also a fact. But so is the enthusiastic response to Tolkien's parable of hope— whether one attributes this to persistent wishful dreaming, or to residual Christianity, or (as Edmund Wilson does) to "a lifelong appetite for juvenile trash." [17] This juxtaposition of facts may itself be a "sign" of some sort. For it is specifically to our world of waning hope, according to his Foreword, that J. R. R. Tolkien presents *The Lord of the Rings*: "to Men of a later Age, one almost as darkling and ominous as was the Third Age that ended with the great years 1418 and 1419 of the Shire long ago."

The Novels of Charles Williams

GEORGE P. WINSHIP, JR.

Charles Williams, like the other writers treated in this volume, was in some sense an amateur novelist: that is, his most evident intentions were not directed toward fiction as such. Critics have on the whole given more attention to his theology or to his rather dense verse. But his seven novels make up an *oeuvre* more considerable in extent and in scope than the production of many an over-deliberate Salinger.

The temptation to judge books in terms of the author's intention is strong and dangerous, as Williams' friend C. S. Lewis has so clearly told us. In reality, the causes of any literary work are many-fold. Let us look at four, following at some distance the four causes named by Aristotle. The author's intention to write at all is an "efficient" cause: at its most respectable, this is to earn money. There is the formal cause: his decision to work in a certain genre, such as the realistic novel, the detective story, or the occult fantasy. There is a material cause: to explain the nature and techniques of warfare, or love, or economics, or witchcraft. And there is the final cause, which if we are hostile we call propaganda: the author's unavoidable need to express what he truly feels. Our judgment of a book depends on our confidence that these four causes operate honestly and independently.

Williams was certainly no amateur in the athletic sense. His friends agree that he always needed money; apparently the Oxford Press paid only a gentlemanly wage. Mrs. Shideler assumes that his novels "sprang from his exuberance in living," [1] but his own explanation was different:

"to pay my son's school fees." To a writer whose natural bent is verse or drama, detective stories and adventure tales do look like a source of income.

The second cause, at least of the early novels, is the form of those commercial genres that he selected. Though far from a standard detective story, as it turns out, *War in Heaven* opens with the discovery of a body and continues with blows on the head and other expected ingredients of a thriller. The publishers have tended to exploit these elements and to treat Williams as if he were more like Graham Greene than he is.[2] Also stereotyped is *Shadows of Ecstasy*, a development of the threat-to-civilization plot. Except that the invasion comes from Africa instead of from Asia or Mars, *Shadows* is another war-of-the-worlds story. One Considine, who seems to be in his vigorous maturity, turns out to be over two hundred years old. He is an adept of many mysteries, including those of jungle sorcerers; and by these means he has drawn the African tribes together to dominate the world. But that is not his principal aim. Rather, having learned longevity, he would experience Resurrection. . . . The plot suggests a sub-literary genre.

But we can be mistaken when we judge by genre. We lump together as "serious novels" fabrications as dissimilar as *The Magic Mountain* and *Atlas Shrugged*, all more or less lineal descendents of *Pamela* and *Tom Jones*. We agree not to call novels some other books, derived from *The Virginian* or *Murders in the Rue Morgue*, let us say. In our public libraries mysteries and westerns are shelved apart. Williams wrote by choice in one or another of the kinds stemming from *The Castle of Otranto*. Some of his admirers admit that he strayed into demesnes unclaimed by Apollo. But he was no lost wanderer. Many intelligent people enjoy writing and reading these genres, which have an artistic discipline on the whole tighter than those of the standard novel. There is nothing to be gained by pretending that Williams was writing the sort of novel produced and talked about by E. M. Forster or Henry James.

But his third cause, the material one, moved Charles

Williams more deeply than did the forms in which he wrote. His material is always fantastic and esoteric, and it is always in some unorthodox way religious. The paradox of his fiction, and I believe the explanation of his hold upon his readers, is simply that for his fantasy he is not content with a willing suspension of disbelief. He demands the destruction of disbelief. Even in *Shadows,* where disbelief is not much defeated, a character contemplates a bookcase and wonders: "If they came alive . . . all shut up in their cases, all nicely shelved—shelved—shelved. We put them in their places in our minds, don't we? If they got out of their bookcases . . . not the charming lines of type but the things the type means. Dare you look for them . . . ?" (p. 44) This very question is the theme of *The Place of the Lion.* The central girl, Damaris Tighe, is compiling a dissertation on Platonic concepts in medieval philosophy. In her view, words and thoughts are things to be manipulated for the sake of an academic degree, and that in turn is sought for the sake of her personal status. But her Nominalism is routed by a peculiarly vivid Realism: the abstract nouns of her philosophy come alive in a series of magnificent beings—Lion, Eagle, Serpent, a Horse that carries a man, a Fire that burns and consumes.

Confronting these, Damaris must stop making use of scholarship and of her lover and accept both as realities. The reader likewise must react to the confrontation. We tell ourselves that a Platonic Idea is not, in plain prose, a visible physical lion, larger and handsomer than life, crystallized about the actual presence of a poor mangy menagerie lioness. In common-sense terms this tale is a fantasy, and in our overbookish world we regard philosophy as something that philosophers write and students take tests on, not as love of wisdom, never as *truth.* But at least we are forced by Williams to think about our thinking. These books are "thrillers"—if that term denotes competent management of suspense. But the thrill is a small thing compared to the washing away of the sandy foundations of our complacency.

Each of Williams' novels is uncanny. In *The Greater*

Trumps there is the same Tarot pack which fascinated Eliot when he wrote *The Waste Land,* the cards that reflect or direct the Great Dance of all that is. These are the true Cards, not the truncated pack of our bridge, poker, and gin, not the greasy cardboards of a fortune-teller, but the originals, with a cunningly-wrought automaton to correspond: the whole device, cards and machine, is powerful not in mere divination but in control of wind and weather, life and death. The book shows an advance in construction, character-drawing, and narrative force. But the most impressive part is the evocation of the Dance that so fascinated the imagination of the Renaissance, as in the *Orchestra* of Sir John Davies. It is the mystery of order in chaos, the puzzle that so concerns our subtlest science today.

> Imagine, then, if you can . . . that everything which exists takes part in the movement of a great dance—everything, the electrons, all growing and decaying things, all that seems alive and all that doesn't seem alive, men and beasts, trees and stones, everything that changes, and there is nothing anywhere that does not change. That change— that's what we know of the immortal dance; the law in the nature of things—that's the measure of the dance, why one thing changes swiftly and another slowly, why there is seeming accident and incalculable alteration, why men hate and love and grow hungry, and cities that have stood for centuries fall in a week . . . there is nothing at all anywhere but the dance. (pp. 94–95)

As we read, we feel that here is not a wildly inventive storyteller but a poet who sees into the heart of matter, side by side with the nuclear physicist. And we may recall that our familiar time-killer, solitaire, is a descendent of sorcery.

Sorcery itself is a major element in Williams' books, and an activity in which he had dabbled. We are assured [3] that he dabbled only. His convenient little volume on witchcraft is based on published sources, not experience. The technical details of black magic which dominate *War in Heaven* and *All Hallows' Eve* are probably discoverable in works of general reference or else invented. But it is a bold scholar who would trace these steps in the dark and tulgey wood of witchcraft. Williams himself was armored with the breastplate of faith, an imaginative as well as a creedal realization of Christianity. Any student who follows him must have in hand a cross; he would be fortunate to carry also the herb moly.

With this precaution, we may examine the goetic elements in Williams' fiction. We encounter sorcery by chalk markings on the floor, by rubbing the skin with ointment distilled from human fat, or by incantation. The latter like all witchcraft is destructive; the adept endeavors to reduce words to mere sounds, much as Shakespeare's Edmund does with "base" and Falstaff with "honour." We meet one magician who yearns to multiply his body so as to act in several places, and Clerk Simon of *All Hallows' Eve* does so. The reunion is destructive and horrible. Sorcery acts against nature; its direction is widdershins, against the sun. Sorcery is cold; Simon's mistress conceives a child intended as a victim and instrument of magic and feels it within her "as cold as spring-water" (p. 101).

Through sorcery the Devil seeks material form, as vainly as he once sought Incarnation in the birth of Merlin. The wizard seeks to produce a semblance of life, molding a dwarfed and misshapen woman from dust and spittle, a habitation for spirits of the dead. Magic is a perverted reflection of Christian sacramentalism. It seeks after power dependent on God's own bridges between spirit and matter, as in its violent struggle in *War in Heaven* for the Holy Graal [sic] discovered in a country church. The cup's custodian, however, is less excited than the magicians: "In one sense, of course, the Graal is unimportant—it is a symbol less near Reality now than any chalice of consecrated wine" (p. 37). In their pursuit of the relic the sorcerers are chasing illusion, as they always do. *Many Dimensions* is another yarn about black magicians and fantastic powers, but the former can originate no control over matter, and the powers all stem from a sacred stone of Suleiman ben Daood (King Solomon), bearing the Name of God. Clerk Simon's daughter, already mentioned, has been brought into the world to be a link between infernal Spirit and redeemed Matter, but heavenly Spirit frustrates that intention. The baby's nurse surreptitiously employs a spell available to the humblest believer and christens the child. Magic exists, but the magic which prevails is white.

If Williams has a point to make, beyond titillation, it is the sacramental one. Spirit and matter really are both God's creatures and belong together. Evil dispositions assume that they are widely separated and may be united only by immense effort, sacrifice, and obscene rites; and these commonly fail in their intended purpose. But they do not fail to carry the soul to destruction, as Gregory Persimmons discovers in *War in Heaven*. Experimenting unsuccessfully in magic, he succeeds in ruining others' lives by temporal means: "Five pounds here, a clever jeer there—it was all easy. Everyone had some security, and he had only to be patient to find and destroy it" (p. 71).

William feeds a persistent human appetite for knowledge without belief. Witchcraft fascinates most of us: the fame of Salem today is not from producing whale oil or shoes. But the fascinated do not believe "seriously" in either sacramentalism or the Devil. Williams attacks unbelief with stories for the unbelieving, to slip under our guard. In this closing passage in *Witchcraft* he speaks of the un–cross-examined evidence in the trials, but what he says is true of his own fiction:

> Underneath all the tales there does lie something different from the tales. How different? In this—that the thing which is invoked is a thing of a different nature, however it may put on a human appearance or indulge in its servants their human appetites. It is cold, it is hungry, it is violent, it is illusory. The warm blood of children and the intercourse at the Sabbath do not satisfy it. It wants something more and other; it wants "obedience," it wants "souls," and yet it pines for matter. It never was, and yet it always is.[4]

Witchcraft exists, as prose fact, if not in the sense supposed by the practitioner, and it is effective, if only for the destruction of the magician's own soul. Sorcery works in the same way that poetry does, by metaphor; and it may be that the evil of witchcraft is like that of bad reading of poetry—the confusion of the figurative with the literal.

Williams shows this in his treatment of the succubus. Satan has always regarded man's sexuality as his most vulnerable point and is ready to provide an infernal mistress. We have hideous glimpses of succubi several times in the verse and prose of Williams, and in *Descent into Hell* one of them plays a large and disturbing role. Wentworth, the character who descends, is a distinguished historian with a following of young people. The middle-aged scholar likes to think himself attractive to one of them, Adela Hunt. Adela, however, is a self-willed and obstinate person, in fact a human being, and to woo her and win her from a rival, Wentworth would have to live actively in the world, to confront people, to strive with other wills and natures—even yield his own wishes at times to theirs. We all have to do this; we may not believe that we have a choice. But Wentworth is given a choice.

He is offered an entirely different Adela, who comes into existence only in response to his appetite, who "lives for him" in the most literal way. She or it talks to him: "You don't think about yourself enough" (p. 82)—but only in the words he wills into its mouth. It fawns upon him. It is light in his arms as he lifts it over the threshhold. It is a sexual instrument, of course, but a sexual partner? It has a frightening resemblance to Catherine and Maria, those succubi in the novels of Hemingway.

When he refuses to struggle even with Adela's own selfishness to possess her, small prize that she is, Wentworth gives up love. Had he made the effort, he might have saved her soul as well as his own. He is content with something less than love and even less than lust, even less than perversion. For perversion means involvement and a sort of love. Peter Stanhope, the wise poet in this novel, identifies Wentworth's spiritual home:

The Lord's glory fell on the cities of the plain, of [sic]
Sodom and another. We know all about Sodom nowadays,
but perhaps we know the other even better. Men can be in
love with men, and women with women, and still be in
love and make sounds and speeches, but don't you know
how quiet the streets of Gomorrah are? haven't you seen
the pools that everlastingly reflect the faces of those who
walk with their own phantasms, but the phantasms aren't
reflected, and can't be. The lovers of Gomorrah are quite
contented. (p. 174)

Even the least disciplined forms of love have something in
them of co-inherence, to use a good word from Williams.
The basest perversions reveal man's yearning toward other
beings or betray his need of them. Except for this one.
Some call it "spiritual incest"; others give it a coarser
name.

The material "cause" here is better known to the poets
than to the theologians. The purely imaginative life is a
precious refreshment but a dangerous refuge. Keats
needed it, explored it, guessed something of its hazards.
The song of the nightingale is a substitute for poisonous
hemlock, or alcohol, or opiates—and Keats was a qualified
medic as well as a poet. His "poesy" does not mean
exactly poetry; it may mean Gomorrah. Magic casements
open upon loveliness; but their seas are "perilous" indeed.
Keats died young; Williams was older and wiser.

Such are the materials which give their particular quality to the novels of Williams. Obscene occultism is especially suitable to convey some of his themes, and perhaps
none of them could have been conveyed with the same
force in a realistic genre with daylight characters.

Let us now examine the fourth element, the group of
final causes of his work. Any author of merit has a number
of things he has to say—living prisoners in the cage of his
imagination. These are causes just as truly as the need for
money, and they determine his destiny as an imaginative
artist. In this instance they touch also the destiny of the
reader.

In general, the theme of Charles Williams is the Christian faith, seen from a rather special and individual point of view. It may be that the majority in nominally Christian countries no longer hold to or even recognize Christian doctrine, although they are sympathetic to what they consider Christian sentiments. Williams confronts his readers with strange assertions and startling images, such as that of the Emperor.

In *The Greater Trumps*, as we have seen, he uses Tarot cards to stand for the correspondences in the real world between natural elements or ideas and human beings. One card is the Emperor, the token on papyrus of Order in the civil realm. A few pages after he appears on the card, a character sees him again as a policeman directing traffic:

> whether something in the policeman's shape and cloak . . . suggested it, or whether indeed something common to Emperor and Khalif, cadi and magistrate, praetor and alcalde, lictor and constable, shone before her . . . it was certainly true that for a moment she saw in that heavy official barring their way the Emperor of the Trumps, helmed, in a white cloak, stretching out one sceptered arm, as if Charlemagne, or one like him, stretched out his controlling sword over the tribes of Europe pouring from the forests and bade them pause or march as he would. (p. 55)

The vision of a disciplined world, to Williams, is a Christian theme. He accepts authority and even hierarchy as consonant with the true nature of things, the same hierarchy that Dante, and before him the so-called Dionysius, delighted to describe in heaven. In his verse Williams used hazel rods as symbols of measurement, of rhythm in verse, and of order generally, including the punishment of unruly servants. Slavery, corporal punishment, and even the authority of the civil police are repellent to the modern liberal imagination, and this revulsion of our society against any manifestation of hierarchy is a condition which not only Christians but elected magistrates must recognize and deal with. It may be that Williams rests too much poetic weight upon the rather trivial figure of a policeman; but the novelist could retort that it is the central task of poetry, especially in the genre of prose fiction, to reveal the deeper implications of the commonplace.

Another final cause is a highly imaginative treatment of time suggesting that time itself is not an absolute reality. Just as the stone of Suleiman ben Daood in *Many Dimensions* defeats space, enabling anyone who possesses it to wish himself anywhere and be there in an instant, so in other books there is travel in time. In *All Hallows' Eve* the principal characters, the dead ones, inhabit Limbo, which as in a sort of slide rule exists concurrently with human time and can touch it at varying points; Simon sends his victim daughter into this Limbo to travel into the future and read the papers for his imformation. But this is trivial magic. More significantly, Williams uses timeless time in *Descent into Hell*. Wentworth's plot in this novel has been discussed; the parallel story concerns Pauline Anstruther, who learns the great doctrine of co-inherence, bearing another's burdens. Stanhope, a poet and an archetype of wisdom, bears a burden for her and she in turn bears one for her own ancestor, dead some four hundred years: John Struther, Protestant martyr in the Marian persecutions. And there is in the book still another exchange between the living and the dead, unhampered by the sequence of time in which we happen to live.

The episodes just mentioned in plot summary are incredible, more preposterous than anything else in these fantastic stories. Even told at full length they are hard to swallow, but Williams means the exchange and perhaps the timelessness as simple and literal truth. Pauline is haunted by a doppelgänger or image of herself. At times she sees herself approaching, and she lives in terror of the day when they, or she, will meet. Her fear threatens her sanity. Stanhope provides a cure. He does not pooh-pooh the girl's belief; he offers to carry her fear, like a parcel,

> when you leave here you'll think of [*sic*] yourself that I've taken this particular trouble over instead of you. You'd do

as much for me if I needed it, or for anyone. And I will give myself to it. I'll think of what comes to you, and imagine it, and know it, and be afraid of it. And then, you see, you won't. (p. 97)

And she doesn't. Indeed, when the doppelgänger meets its original, it in turn effects an exchange; the image speaks the words to the ancestral martyr, "Give it to me, John Struther" (p. 170). Stanhope does not destroy the aberration but he carries the fear. Here is an element of doctrine that Williams shared with Lewis: it is not the event provoking an emotion that is a spiritual danger, but the emotion itself. Williams maintains that emotions can not only be confided in others but exchanged with them.

This is co-inherence, Williams' most characteristic teaching. All men are brothers in more than a genetic or merely integrationist sense; he believes that when we are commanded to bear one another's burdens our Lord means us to support one another in the most intimate possible way. The type example, as the Lion is the type of all lions and of all strength, is the Substitution on the Cross.

The co-inherence of souls separated by time, or even of souls separated as individual people, is not according to common sense. John is not Sally; I am not you. We are brought up to admire independence and to feel that every man should stand on his own two feet. But common sense is not, perhaps, the last word; scientists teach that time is merely a dimension, like height and length. And if Christianity is true it would seem that individuality is analogous to merely a dimension of our existence. Lewis, commenting on Williams, says this:

> The Atonement was a substitution . . . [and] far from being a mere legal fiction . . . was simply the supreme instance of a universal law. "He saved others, himself he cannot save" is a *definition* of the Kingdom. All salvation . . . is vicarious. . . . No man can paddle his own canoe and every man can paddle his fellow's. . . . This Williams most seriously maintained, and I have reason to believe that he spoke from experimental knowledge.[5]

Ultimately we all depend upon one another. There is a significant expansion of a cliché in *Descent into Hell*; the speakers are Stanhope and Lily Sammile (Adam's first tempter; an emissary of the Evil One):

> "I must go," she said. "But I don't see why you don't enjoy yourselves."
>
> "Because, sooner or later, there isn't anything to enjoy in oneself." (p. 64)

The final cause of all—not what Williams teaches, let us say, but what he studies—is what can save the soul. Obedience can save it; had Adela Hunt been able to douse her pride in an affectionate relationship to her dominating young man she would have escaped the hell which closes in on her at the end. Joy can save it, joy in another man's honor or benefit. Astonishingly, another salvation lies in hatred, if it is the honest scholar's hatred for inaccuracy (*Descent*, pp. 38, 80, 197, and 215). Hatred is not pretty, but what counts in life as in art is not beauty but truth. All that truly is, is of God. Williams describes the Thames, recalling by contrast a famous passage in *The Waste Land*,

> The river ran . . . heavily with the weight of its mirk. . . . Twigs, bits of paper and wood, cords, old boxes drifted on it. . . . The dirtiness of the water was, at that particular point, what it should be and therefore pleasant enough. The evacuations of the City had their place in the City; how else could the City be the City? Corruption (so to call it) was tolerable, even adequate and proper, even glorious. These things also were facts. They could not be forgotten or lost in fantasy; all that had been, was; all that was, was. A sodden mass of cardboard and paper drifted by, but the soddenness was itself a joy, for this was what happened, and all that happened, in this great material world, was good. (*All Hallows' Eve*, pp. 196–97)

The character appreciates the material world so much because she is dead; but the living Anthony in *The Place of the Lion* sees the world with the same joy:

How firmly the houses were set within the ground! with what decision each row of bricks lay level upon the row beneath! Spires and towers and chimneys thrust into the sky, and slender as they were, it was an energetic slenderness. The trees were drawing up strength and displaying it, and the sunlight communicated strength. The noises that came to him from the street resolved themselves into a litany of energy. (pp. 155–56)

Williams loved the literal as he did the theological City; the visible world, with more of people than Wordsworth liked, gave him a Wordsworthian delight. The dead and living characters who look upon these scenes are saved. This author's fantasies come from a brain which had no quarrel with Creation.

It has been argued (with a "perhaps") that the passage of time is not an ultimate reality, that exchange between persons is possible, that materialism is not true. The "perhaps" is necessary: our scientific education presses upon us, as does the deceptive common sense of every day. We cannot "know" hell and heaven except by the testimony of our emotions. But that testimony can be denied or confirmed by the witness of other lives in literature; the expert authorities upon emotions are the poets.

So it is especially important to know whether such a witness as Charles Williams is truly a poet. It has been charged with sneers that he is not; in cross-examination it is charged that his credentials have been forged by fellow Christians and by personal friends. It is too bad if a man must be blamed for friendship, but indeed we who read him are few enough to be called a clique.

We cannot assert his authenticity by the evidence of his style. When he writes at his best, which is magnificently, it is in passages of such strange, uncanny action that when quoted in isolation they sound simply bad. More mundane pages are usually clear, but not always: astonishingly for a professional editor, Williams has some trouble with grammar. On the larger scale of structure he is better, although he learned slowly how to compose a novel. The later stories are admirably planned. The symmetry of paired characters in *The Greater Trumps* and *Descent into Hell* evinces a firm sense of design. Characterization is perhaps not important in stories of this particular type, but he has one rare excellence. It is recognized that good people are the most difficult to create in fiction and that Williams excels in presenting sanctity. But surely his greatest talent, and that upon which his authority as an honest witness must rest, is his ability to present to our imagination what is denied by our presuppositions, to make real what lies beyond reality.

Most of us who have written about him have apologized for what we feel is not serious fiction. "Serious" is a convenient word in common speech, but it is not very useful for exact thought. A tale can of course be serious in the sense of solemn, as have been most novels in the central sociological tradition. It may be direct rather than ironic. It may be honest with its normal reader. It may be written with artistic integrity rather than out of contempt for the genre itself—in meretricious imitation of other men's honest work. It may be written well. When we say "serious" we do not examine very closely which we mean. But we ought not to mean simply fashionable, in the "great tradition," in a majority genre. In a fantastic type ignored by most literary critics two classics are recognized, *Brave New World* and *1984*, one comic and one solemn, both honest and written well, both serious. Readers of the present volume will surely accept Lewis's interplanetary stories as serious. The ghost genre includes at least *The Turn of the Screw*. Charles Williams is full of lessons, and one that we should not ignore is a warning against literary snobbery.

The Relationship of Charles Williams' Working Life to His Fiction

ALICE MARY HADFIELD

Charles Williams' office life was always on the point of becoming the opening of one of his own novels. Every morning when I went to work I had a fluttering feel that it might happen, and although my office was on the floor below I would make sure I got into the plot.

The most essential thing was that we were in London. Five of the seven novels open in London: *Descent into Hell* and *The Place of the Lion* open in a small place satellite to London, and Anthony and Quentin of *The Place of the Lion* live and work in London. We were totally surrounded by city streets, crowds, noise, people, buses and cars. "Only a few devout followers of Wordsworth can in fact find more than mere quiet in the country" (*The Place of the Lion*, chap. 9, par. 1). London was where life happened, the seat of the soul, the scene of war (*All Hallows' Eve*), of the African ecstasy of black power, framework of the spiritual city (*All Hallows' Eve*), the place to which you returned after getting upset by your young man or your family in the country.

Then there was work—books, manuscripts, authors, publishers, printers and binders, managers of production, of countinghouse, stock, publicity and reviews, American universities' publications. This was a field of natural contest in which C. W. took a full part. Dropping into his office at any moment I would find him reverberating down the telephone about reprints of the Oxford Standard Authors, or stonily refusing to include a defective version of an alternative line of the *Prelude,* or passionately pointing out priority to printers. The accuracy and feeling with which the interaction of Caithness, Considine and Sir Bernard is handled in Chapters 2, 6 and 7 of *Shadows of Ecstasy* reflects his own experience. Every moment was liable to show spiritual powers stalking in the office. This was what we junior fry revelled in.

C. W. was not inclined to feel that they stalked much in schools, colleges, churches, except as these were places of man's necessary paid employment. Work and home were the centers of power. Anything could be, but the commonplace and the necessary were always vehicles of the extraordinary. In his experience, the extraordinary always used the commonplace, and once the extraordinary was recognized in the situation one's sights were raised and all extraordinary developments could be accepted and assimilated in the manner of the commonplace. Look in *The Greater Trumps,* at the car journey (chap. 4), where the ordinary street sights are objects of another order of significance, and the ordinary becomes extraordinary without any outward order of significance when the car is suddenly halted by—only an old woman in the middle of the road. Or Chapter 1 of *War in Heaven* where the sub-editor finds a man under his desk and the man turns out to be a corpse. Or Chapter 1 of *The Place of the Lion,* when the frontier between commonplace and extraordinary sways to and fro—a circus and an escaped animal, or qualities taking animal form without possibility of control? And the cry of the old seer in Chapter 2 of *The Greater Trumps,* who saw the day of fate shown in the cards and did not recognize it—"Did yesterday promise nothing for today?" the young man asked. "Nothing that I thought important. Something was to come to you. . . . What *could* I think? It was a day's chance." Or Chapter 9 of *War in Heaven*: "So through the English roads the Graal was borne away in the care of a Duke, an Archdeacon, and a publisher's clerk, pursued by a country householder, the Chief Constable of a county, and a perplexed policeman."

The convincing point in this aspect of the novels has always been to me the knowledge from office experience that C. W. believed in the commonplace. He did not put up with it, or explain it or try to get away from it. He believed in it, committed his mind to it, and so came into its possibilities. Therefore it was as natural to talk to him about my landlady, rent, lodging, my mother's little ways, our old cat, as about love, literature or money. Chapter 6 of *The Greater Trumps* contains conversation between Aaron the seer and his grandson about Sybil. The intent old man says, "She's merely commonplace—a fool, and the sister of a fool." Later, speaking of desire and fulfillment, he says, "And has Sybil Coningsby carried out her desire? What was it then?" His grandson answers, "I can't tell you, but she found it and she stands within it, possessing it perfectly. Only she doesn't know what she's done." In the same book, Nancy moves in the development of love from not possessing it in herself and not knowing what she is doing to possessing and knowing, and along that line she finds extraordinary experiences and behavior natural to her.

One of the many developments of this committal to the commonplace is a conviction about government, order and society. Neither of the figures of power which C. W. explored in *Shadows of Ecstasy*, or *All Hallows' Eve*, had this committal or this conviction. Nor did the lion, snake or horse of *The Place of the Lion*, nor the deniers or sceptres of *The Greater Trumps*, nor the stones of the ring of Suleiman in *Many Dimensions* when they were active in human society. But the life of the blessed was a life of free order and joy. In *All Hallows' Eve*, Chapter 9, Lester, now far on the same development as Nancy in *The Greater Trumps*, though after death instead of before, looks at the city of London at the busy area of Blackfriars, and the river crowded with traffic and tidal debris: "To her now all states of being were beginning to be of their own proper kind, each in itself and in its relationships, and not hampering the vision of others." Chapter 16 of *The Place of the Lion* shows a restoration of order to the ideas in animal form and the exchange of obedience between Damaris and Anthony. Chapter 10 in *Descent into Hell* presents the sound of the trumpet and consummation of experience as near to the unpresentable and inapprehensible as one might go, but there is "mutual perception," there is "justice" (meaning an order, proportion), there is knowledge—and these things are not nirvana or anarchy or annihilation.

C. W. did not practise approaches to nirvana or anarchy in the office. In a big publishing house he moved among all grades exactly as Lester saw London's city and river, knowing the stock boys who brought copies from stock shelves, assistants who had been in the Bible and Prayer Book showroom almost as long as the century, the publisher in his absoluteness, the telephone girl in the hall in her omniscience, his equals the specialist editors, the head of music, of juvenile publications, the librarian, me the new girl, knowing and thereby maintaining our identities and our differences. If his touch faltered, it was in veneration and fear of a manual worker, as he showed in Chapter 1 of *War in Heaven* when Lionel assumes that the man under the desk is repairing the telephone and spends three paragraphs collecting the nerve to deal with him.

He was helped by the organization of the firm, which had no editorial office which warred as one with production or publicity. The editors were specialists and worked on their own. Although for years C. W. shared an office with Fred Page, accuracy specialist and expert on Patmore, when I joined the firm he had a slice of a room to himself. So he was never responsible for the well-being or the actions of a group of staff. He had one personal assistant, Ralph Binfield, whom he sent to the British Museum to check the text of Oxford Standard Authors or set to make indexes. The responsibility of department empire-building was never his. His relationships therefore could remain personal and literary.

Which plane corrected which, I do not know, but the fact remains that no one knew better than C. W. what could be done and what could not. The terms an author could ask, the degree to which a publisher's agreement could be enforced, the composition of a dramatic club's committee, the awards to expect from arbitration on a strike, the peace terms which you could expect to read in the paper after a war, the odds for or against asking for a Friday afternoon off, nobody questioned that C. W. was the man to have a word with on these. He had a most acute sensitiveness to how the world works, and could set aside your own urgent self-delusions calmly and without fuss. If you stormed out and ignored his advice, the worse for you in the result. Look at *War in Heaven*, Chapter 4, paragraph beginning "The first thing that occurred to him was the bank; the second was the Bishop."

C. W. was a man of his generation, and believed in politics and government. He preferred the wrangles of democracy to the placidity of well-kept children varied by assassination which he saw as a likely alternative. He always held that the democratic process had a long way further to go, and often quoted G. K. Chesterton's poem "The Secret People": "We are the people of England, and we have not spoken yet. Smile at us, pay us, pass us. But do not quite forget." How swiftly does his imagination leap from the first loosing of non-human power upon society to the straightforward means of controlling or forwarding it, by the county or national channels of authority! By Chapter 2 in *Shadows of Ecstasy* the affair was in the headlines of the daily papers, reporting army and government announcements. Chapter 3 is concerned with the pronouncement of the African High Executive, Chapter 7 with an interview with the Prime Minister, Chapter 9 with the African High Executive, and Chapter 10 with the breakdown of public order in London. In *Many Dimensions*, there is the Persian Ambassador in Chapter 1, a permanent official of the Foreign Office in Chapter 3, the Foreign Secretary in Chapter 7, while the hero of the book is the Lord Chief Justice. Part of the action in Chapter 8 takes place in the conference at the Foreign Office. Chapter 12 is occupied with the General Secretary of the National Transport Union and a manager of an Airways Company, and Chapter 16 with the decisions of the Home Secretary and the Foreign Secretary. There is hardly any touch of satire in all this, though occasionally of amusement. A more unusual figure in English writing is the Mayor of the town of Rich, an office which appealed to C. W. as being directly elected by the people of any place and not politically connected with national parties. C. W. is probably the only poet who has celebrated Christ as the young Lord Mayor, in "Celestial Cities," a poem in his early book, *Divorce*.

Part of this positive attitude towards society was his good capacity for relationships. He had a warm friendship with his father, a long care and attention towards his mother, and an affectionate and reliable friendship with his sister. Although there are tremors of irritability in the family life scenes of *The Greater Trumps*, Chapters 1, 3, and 4, there is nothing basically poisonous in the relationship; each member acts from it, and it develops into part of the renewed life of each one at the end. So too in *War in Heaven*, Chapters 2 and 11. In *Descent into Hell*, Pauline's development works through her life with her grandmother, and family relationship is found capable of operating towards an ancestor of four hundred years ago.

C. W. also enjoyed the companionship of men. In his young time he had a deep and happy friendship with Harold Eyers and Ernest Nottingham. The conversations and the weekend walks, sometimes for half the night, are part of his early *Poems of Conformity*. Later on there was Daniel Nicholson, and all through C. W.'s life he thoroughly enjoyed conversation, a lunch, a drink, a theater, with other men. As his life gradually surrounded him with young students from his lectures, he appreciated men of his own age even more. He would very often have lunch with men from other publishing firms whom he had met over some committee, or who had written to him about an article in a magazine. Eliot from Faber and Faber was often among these.

A good reflection of this enjoyment is the pleasure and kinship which sparks up between Anthony and Richardson in *The Place of the Lion*. So with the first meeting of Kenneth and the Duke of the North Ridings in *War in Heaven*. Evelyn in *Descent into Hell* is a figure of a destructive relationship, friendship reversed, which shows up the true nature of friendship by defining its absence. And of course Evelyn had no conversation.

To exchange and explore ideas in talk was pretty well the noblest work of man to C. W.—always excepting to live them. But he preferred the fellow who could talk about them as well. No monologuist, he never lectured off the rostrum. He did not dominate a conversation, though he might transform it. Often my worst moments were recalling my own voice explaining something to C. W. The characteristic sound coming out of an office where C. W. was in conversation was the explosion of words from the other people. Even an official committee would emit a shout of laughter, and was usually heard breaking up in a clatter of voices and amusement so that we all knew C. W. was free. Indeed, an exchange of ideas was the essence of his love of conversation. People whom he called "pillar-boxes," into whom he continually posted talk without getting any response except pleased listening, soon ceased to give him any pleasure, though he never "dropped" people. He often remarked that the people who were most up in art and literature were the most like this, because they talked always impersonally and used culture as a specialist "subject," so that experience never struck fire out of talk on poetry or painting. This was always other men's expression. He complained once about a man who was an expert on modern novels: "The fellow never says 'When my wife threw me out in the night last January I saw what Faulkner, or Cary or so on, really meant, etc.'" *Shadows of Ecstasy* was his first novel (published later) and shows most clearly of them all his protest against using literature and not living it. Before Sartre or Mauriac, Roger Ingram speaks in Chapter 2 of his Chair of Applied Literature as an embalming workshop, and his lectures as exhibiting the embalmed body to visitors at so much a head. C. W.'s conviction was expressed in Chapter 1, that criticism was still an almost undiscovered art, being a final austere harmony produced by the purification of literature from everything alien. Things alien included arranging works and lines in order of merit, making systems of chronology, subject, meter or familiarity, every activity with literature except studying the life in the lines themselves. It was this kind of criticism which made his writing on the most worn subjects remarkable—Shakespeare, Milton, Wordsworth. It was this above all things which drew people to him in his evening classes and in the last great years in his lectures at Oxford. Life, and power, and holy fear sprang in our hearts at his exposition. As Roger Ingram says in Chapter 7 of *Shadows of Ecstasy*, there was power and we hungered to feel it live. I have known love and war and death, but echoes of C. W.'s invocation of power in *King Lear, The Prelude, Paradise Lost, Macbeth*, stand as strong as they.

In *Descent into Hell* the slant on the same matter is different, being written from the point of view of the poet expressing power rather than exposing it. C. W. had a full experience on this angle in the ten years or so when he was writing plays for local groups. One play, *Cranmer of Canterbury*, had a near professional start, but *Judgment at Chelmsford, Seed of Adam, The House by the Stable, Death of Good Fortune, The House of the Octopus*, were committed to keen small groups, whose zeal was often concerned with things alien from literature. C. W. enjoyed the work and the rehearsals immensely, and even if he smiled or sighed now and then, as did Stanhope in *Descent into Hell*, Chapters 1, 4, 6, and 8, there was always something found of the nature suddenly triumphant in Chapter 10. The *Masques* which he wrote for fun and saw performed in Amen House in the early days of his power were the purest and most enchanting discoveries of power.

Half the strength of his writing and speaking was lucidity and accuracy, both of observation and of expression.

He was always lucid. He could explain a copyright position to a production conference or a percentage position
to an author, or dispute a plagiarism with a cunning
magazine editor. See how he handles movement in time
in *Many Dimensions*, Chapter 6. He could also most
distressingly expose one's real motive during one's best
build-up. That a situation, large or small, should be so and
not otherwise was always of interest to him, and he had
very little interest in illusions, disguises or mistakes.
Truth, fact, the nature of the universe demonstrated in
every facet of life, was the absorbing thing, and he made
any facet of our lives absorbing. Essential to its study was
the ability to realize that one had been, or was, just plain
wrong, and to admit it. This is a moment in Damaris'
redemption, in *The Place of the Lion*, Chapter 9, and a
step on Chloe's way in *Many Dimensions*, Chapter 14, a
moment of foreboding awareness in Nancy in *The
Greater Trumps*, Chapter 8. Another side of the ability is
flashed in a phrase in Chapter 10 of *The Greater Trumps*,
"It is only the right steps we have to mind." Deriving
from this, C. W. was often impatient with books which
were content to build up to huge or sordid tragedy and
leave this as the final message. In *The Greater Trumps*,
Chapter 10, when Nancy discovers that Henry has been
trying to kill her father, she has a natural despair and
prostration. Sybil handles her most lovingly, and in the
course of it says, "I'll see to your father, and you see to
Henry. Do let's get on to important things." No remark
brings C. W. more clearly to mind's eye. So Nancy gets
herself back to the work of loving, gets Henry back, and
gets on with the story.

All the novels have a brilliance of clear movement,
often far from simple, both of the author's thinking and
in the action of the story. *Many Dimensions* and *The
Place of the Lion* are particularly so, perhaps because they
deal more with facts than ideas, more with stones, hours,
movement, theft, lions, butterflies, eagles, pterodactyls,
college degrees, lectures, strength, speed, control, than
with perception, sacrifice, exchange, conquests of death,

the nature of another life. C. W. certainly thought, and often said, that accuracy marked the way to heaven and inaccuracy to hell. All cherished illusions and blurrings of distinction allowed the mind to see things otherwise than as they were, and hell was in his view not so much an imposed judgment as an exclusion from real life or the nature of heaven. The figure of Sir Bernard in *Shadows of Ecstasy* is very close to C. W. himself, delighting in the exact shape of events and motives, delighting in his delight.

Accuracy did not mean condemning one or approving the other, or demanding action to follow on an opinion. No one was less likely to start a crusade, or join one, than C. W. In *Descent into Hell*, Chapter 2, he ponders the total lack of joy in the workman's life, in many lives, the resulting suicide, the continued joylessness without the escape of death. There is no feeling that it is the fault of their education, or feeding, or parents or society. C. W. believed that the ills of society, as of health, lay within the nature of man and were in any generation both curable and incurable. Some evils decreased while others increased, the struggle had to go on, but was never hopeless.

He spoke very little about religion, or any particular practice of belief, though we knew he was an Anglican and went to church. The Methodist service in the Zion chapel, Chapter 12 of *The Place of the Lion*, is the most sympathetically treated religious episode in the novels, followed by the Anglican service at the end of *War in Heaven*. The Communion service of exorcism in *Shadows of Ecstasy* is austere, but impressive, though Ian Caithness the priest is ruthless and self-willed. The most attractive and interesting of all the ecclesiastical figures is the Archdeacon, keeper of the Graal in *War in Heaven*, the man who saw that his work was not to defend the Graal but to preserve its freedom, not to defend God but to remain in Him. C. W. understood natural, instinctive religion far more truly than do many students of religion or psychology. In *War in Heaven*, Chapter 12, the villain Gregory

Persimmons has it, and C. W. appreciated it: "Of all those who lay awake under those midnight stars, he was the only one who had a naturally religious spirit. . . . Prayer was natural to him as it was not to Sir Giles or Lionel." C. W. admired people like this as innocent or intrepid scientists who would study the nature of an erupting volcano. He would say to a colleague who was talking of the need to show love and goodwill in public or business dealings with other people, "And would you *like* it? *You,* you would show *love* to the Counting-House? *You* think of showing goodwill to the editor of the T.L.S.?" Or, in a hollow voice, "Do you honestly realize, dear fellow, what it would mean to you, or to me, to be made conformable to love? For all our sakes, don't go praying, or do anything to bring this frightful process on us before we need."

His concept of the City in the last chapter of *All Hallows' Eve* is a fore-thinking to the churchless religion of our times. Throughout all the novels the implication is clear of religion, or experience with and worship of God, diffused in all men and not depending on any channel, not even benefiting by a channel. In his poem "The Prayers of the Pope," in *The Region of the Summer Stars,* the instituted household is ceremonially dissolved and spirit and practice acknowledged to be dispersed among all and the responsibility of each. One person may mediate the practice to another, as in marriage, as in Stanhope to Pauline in *Descent into Hell,* as Betty to Lester in *All Hallows' Eve,* as C. W. to some young and older women and men — but only for a time, only acknowledged constantly as a temporary channel of the true knowledge of God. Even so, C. W. was a prophet in this as in his deeper visions, for he wrote before the unchurching of Christ became a public issue, and though he did not write in terms of how it might be done, yet he thought in terms of it already done. Even Kierkegaard was yet unknown in England, and as I have shown elsewhere, C. W. was the man who opened the door to the publishing of Kierkegaard in England.

The novels deal lavishly with love, love between men and women, but they don't deal with sex and they don't deal with sentiment. This is just like C. W.'s life in his office. We always knew to a T whose office doors we had better knock on (I don't suppose the owners knew how clearly the public in the office knew), but C. W.'s was never one of these. I might barge in on an enclosure of particular stillness, find a person sitting on the hard chair the other side of the desk and C. W. walking up and down the narrow path between his desk and the wall shelves of Oxford Poets and Standard Authors, or sitting on the corner of his desk, smoking—but the eyes which came round to mine were looking on inner truth or trouble, not concerned with detection and concealment. So Stanhope conducted intercourse and exchange with Pauline in *Descent into Hell*, and Lord Arglay with Chloe in *Many Dimensions*, or Jonathan with Richard in *All Hallows' Eve*. C. W. possessed chastity, without consciousness or pressure. He was a married man and a father, and in no sense sealed off. The physical form of woman and man held his whole attention (except for the unimaged adoration of God) and not the sexual activity only. He appreciated that; it has its place through all the rhythmic pulse of *Shadows of Ecstasy*, and through all the devious twilight of Wentworth and Lily Sammile in *Descent into Hell*. But what is the centre of power, of original discovery in *Shadows of Ecstasy*? Philip's knowledge of Rosamond's body in Chapters 4 and 6: "he had seen the verge of a great conclusion of mortal things . . . abysses of intelligence lay beyond it, . . . a bar of firmamental power across the whole created universe, dividing and reconciling at once." In a late unpublished poem he wrote that "the central neural spasm" distracts from that profound study. To him that spasm was only part of the study, and the modern dissection of the sexual impulses in public and in person was shallow and repetitive.

He had many relationships and friendships, and a large part of all of them was conducted by letter. Talking of a Last Judgment, he once said that a fearful part of it would necessarily be a simultaneous knowledge by all of all one's words spoken and written, but that he believed that no two women would be able to confound him by showing that he had said or written exactly the same phrase to each one. So in *All Hallows' Eve,* Chapter 2, Jonathan "never said the same thing to two people; something similar perhaps, but always distinguished, though occasionally hardly anyone but he could distinguish the distinction." Since that time, I have seen a quantity of letters and poems C. W. wrote to other young women, as to me, and this was perfectly true.

He was deeply concerned with each and all of us, but he was not concerned with his relationship to any of us. The women he liked were of the Chloe Burnett mind, quick to catch fire at an image or an idea. Static or self-involved people like Damaris Tighe, Rosamond Murchison or Lawrence Wentworth were a burden which he bore till he could put it down. He would think and talk and explore the nature of things with anyone who would come on the way. The early novels contain a central character which bases itself on detachment from belief and from close ties, while encouraging all good life—Sir Bernard in *Shadows of Ecstasy,* Lord Arglay in *Many Dimensions.* By the time of *Descent into Hell,* 1937, Stanhope lives from a totally different base. He is committed yet free, involved in Pauline without being her lover, her father-figure or her hero, in a changed manner which could only arise from development in the experience of the writer.

C. W. grew on from detachment, and found that some acceptances gave more than they took. For many years he had a horror of immortality, of any continuation of consciousness. He seemed to desire no personal God and no continuing relationship with one. In Chapter 1 of *Descent into Hell,* the first introduction of Stanhope at the reading of his play is a close resemblance to C. W. himself. It is not all that attractive. But the last chapter shows blood in the man. In C. W.'s last years I heard him ponder the smallness of his knowledge, and the instinct that there must be more to know, and that this more must be known and therefore desired to be known, and therefore that life after death could be acceptable.

The last novel, *All Hallows' Eve*, published in the year he died, is a flourish of non-detachment, of committal of every kind and every shade, and an implicit consent to the continuing of life after death. There is one poignant little passage which throws a shaft of light:

> Her heart was tranquil. If she must go, she must go; perhaps this hovering flicker of known joy might be permitted to go with her. All that was noble in her lifted itself in that moment. The small young figure before her was her judge; but it was also the centre and source of the peace.

Both his final non-fiction, *The Figure of Arthur*, and poetry, *The Region of the Summer Stars*, show a sustained increase of power in the person of the writer, an increase which made his early death at fifty-eight so great a loss.

Christian Doctrine and the Tactics of Romance
The Case of Charles Williams

W. R. IRWIN

There is no need to prove that Charles Williams' seven works of prose fiction are romances dedicated to the propagation of the faith. Critics and common readers have always accepted them as such. But published studies of Williams show an imbalance—preponderant concern with the doctrine, near neglect of the literary form and tactics. Thus commentators, sometimes his proponents, expose his fiction to the charge often brought against the *roman à thèse*, that it is a monster made of disparities, even less coherent than minotaur or hippogriff.

One need be no extravagant admirer to maintain that the works of Williams do not merit the condemnation. Indeed, far from being assembled disparities, doctrine and narrative in his romances regularly interact to support and illuminate each other. In this respect his work is part of a long tradition in fiction in which art and rhetoric, often thought enemies, are in fact allies. To demonstrate the interdependence in Williams' fiction is the intent of this essay.

It will be advantageous first to review the central doctrines which Williams wishes to urge. This will be only a brief rehearsal of Christian tenets which in his view should be familiar to all. He intended no innovation; indeed, innovation would be hostile to his purposes. Rather he wished to reassert eternal Providence, the nature and workings of which have been nearly forgotten in an age which serves Mammon, mistakenly believing that it serves itself or a life-force. Like C. S. Lewis, Williams was an advocate of "classical Christianity."

In all of Williams' romances there is a sustained concern with the uses of power, and in five—*War in Heaven, Many Dimensions, The Greater Trumps, Shadows of Ecstasy,* and *All Hallows' Eve*—this is the center of conflict. Williams has no startling word about the nature of power. It simply is, of itself morally neutral. Without advancing any argument, he opposes the widespread notion, popularized in the apothegm of Lord Acton, that power is intrinsically corrupting. For Williams, as for orthodox Christian morality, the issue lies rather in the uses and abuses.

The principle of discrimination between use and abuse is simplicity itself. Those who receive power without seeking, sometimes without knowing that they have it, and exercise it in humility and charity, become beneficent super-beings. Because their will conforms to divine will, they cannot be defeated, even though fearsomely opposed. Their reward is serenity in earthly life and presumably paradise thereafter. Those, however, who snatch power and try to use it for their own ends become monsters and destroyers. They cause widespread misery and what may appear frustration of divine will, but they cannot achieve their ultimate wishes. If they do not destroy themselves, the agents of the divine in time will destroy them. The Manichaean heresy receives no hearing in the romances of Charles Williams.

In three of the works named above the evil attempts at unlimited power center on possession of a power-giving object. In *War in Heaven* it is the Grail; in *Many Dimensions,* the magical stone, from the crown of Suleiman ben Daood of Jerusalem, which bears the characters of the Tetragrammaton; in *The Greater Trumps,* the original Tarot deck. In *Shadows of Ecstasy* a self-proclaimed inheritor of the mantle of Caesar aspires to political domination of Europe by commanding (as he claims) the energies of a blood-dimmed tide stored up in Africa. *All Hallows' Eve* shows us a diabolical campaign for the possession of souls, a kind of power always gratifying to the Enemy. In each instance, the purpose is unlawful aggrandizement or revenge against the good (often the same thing); in each instance the early manifestations of evil are awesome, but its end impotent.

Certain other doctrines, presumably favorites with Williams, are closely associated with his representations of the nature and uses of power. He was fond of the concept of co-inherence, and in his hands it has a remarkable variety. The spiritual is immanent in the physical, as a fact more than as a means of allegory. Separations resulting from acceptance of conventional time and space are abolished. Instead, past, present, and future become one; the dead and the living inhabit the same world and act in it freely, often upon each other. Many of Williams' characters are of the present time, but he does not hesitate to introduce among them Simon Magus, Prester John (a plausible young man in gray flannel who claims oneness also with John the Baptist, Mary, and Galahad), or the nature-mastering Adam reincarnate in one Anthony Durrant. Freedom from the finitude of time and space is a feature of Williams' worlds, in which there is little discrimination between the commonplace and the miraculous. Indeed, he says, in effect, as did Blake, that the commonplace contains and expresses the miraculous. T. S. Eliot's comment on Williams himself applies to this unitive aspect of his work:

> For him there was no frontier between the material and the spiritual world. . . . To him the supernatural was perfectly natural, and the natural was also supernatural. And this peculiarity gave him that profound insight into Good and Evil, into the heights of Heaven and the depths of Hell, which provides both the immediate thrill and the permanent message of his novels.[1]

The moral dimension of his insistence on co-inherence is that serenity, even paradise, resides in active Christian charity, as hell resides in assertive egocentricity. Charity brings together even the repugnant. His version of charity

little resembles the natural affections cherished by benev-
olists and sentimentalists. For Williams charity is much
more an achievement than an endowment. It must be
developed from goodness against opposition from within
and without. That is to say, charity is a virtue and an
obligation, the rewards of which repay the effort which it
costs. The specific manifestation of charity which Williams delights to show is the bearing of one another's
burdens. Thus, in *Descent into Hell*, the saintly poet
Peter Stanhope takes on Pauline's fear of her doppelgänger, just as she takes on her martyred ancestor's fear
of the flames. These heroic actions result from honoring
what Williams called "the central mystery of Christen-
dom, the terrible fundamental substitution." [2]

The doctrine which Williams chose to illustrate in
fiction is neither systematic nor exhaustive. No professional theologian, he concentrated on those aspects of
Christian theology which were, one supposes, most congenial to his imagination and most adaptable to his art. It
must be noted, however, that he stresses the unitive nature of creation and divine purpose. The abuses of power
divide, subjugate, alienate; its proper uses bring human
wills into harmony with each other and with the divine.

There is, then, a kind of reduction to fundamental
belief throughout the principles on which Williams bases
his fiction. This carries directly into his conduct of narrative, determining characterization and action. An examination of his methods will reveal the relationships.

In a general article on Williams' romances George P.
Winship notes that the characters reflect "a dualistic
philosophy embodying good or evil rather than the mix-
ture which has become the norm in the modern novel." [3]
This is certainly true; indeed, it might be expected. The
nature of romance invites portrayals of absolutes rather
than highly individualized persons. As Northrop Frye has
demonstrated, characters in romance usually owe their
being and energy to a principle or allegiance which has
been somewhat internalized rather than to any originally
inner prompting.[4] One does not look to romance for a

probing of the psyche and emotions. Henry Fielding discriminated between unilateral characters and mixed, and saw the propriety of the latter for the new mode in prose fiction which he helped to establish. Others followed, extended, and developed his perception. But romance has never disappeared, and with it has persisted monistic characterization, convenient for embodying types and undifferentiated principles. Now Williams made an effort to give personality to some of his characters by providing details of appearance, attitude, habit, opinion, indeed of almost every source of personal distinctiveness except plausible speech, for he seems to have had little talent in dialogue. These remain, however, superficial, and his few memorable characters are so because of the significance which they bear rather than because the meaning which by their fullness of development they give to the entire work. The organic art by which Stendhal and Dostoevsky educed universal significance from individualized characters was seemingly beyond Williams, as was the complementary art which produced the questing Dante or Christian the pilgrim. For one example, Sir Giles Tumulty, who is prominent as a disturber of the peace in *War in Heaven* and *Many Dimensions*, is a Faust-figure, endowed with all the appropriate associations. But as a person Sir Giles lacks the grandeur, audacity, and speculative capability of his prototype. He is as real as Falstaff in love.

But such characterization, however lacking in comparison with the triumphs of narrative history, serves Williams' purpose well. His human participants are usually of two kinds: those whose knowledge and endowments give them a special and understood objective, for good or evil, from the beginning; and those ordinary mortals who, at least early in their involvement, find themselves caught in an incomprehensible turmoil of events. Of the first kind, the figures are often mythical or legendary, or, if contemporary, have the qualities of such. I have mentioned Prester John and Simon Magus; there are also Nigel Considine, Lord Arglay, Hajji Ibrahim, and others. The second kind have no great names or accomplishments, but they are just as much agents of superhuman power. Of these, T. S. Eliot remarks,

> He [Williams] sees the struggle between Good and Evil as carried on, more or less blindly, by men and women who are often only the instruments of higher or lower powers, but who always have the freedom to choose to which powers they will submit themselves.[5]

This is true enough, but I must emphasize that, as they exercise choice, characters who are at first ignorant and remain humble may gain a power which is almost transcendent, as, for example, does Chloe Burnett in *Many Dimensions*. She is a secretary of no great personal endowment, but, with an extraordinary capability of submitting her will to valid authority, she becomes an agent of salvation.

Just as characters in Williams' fiction are determined by allegiance, so is the progress of action. The basis is, of course, the warfare of good and evil, and the movement of warfare follows a standard pattern. Early in the action the aggressions or assertions of evil move rapidly, almost unchecked, whereas the proponents of good are slow and confused. Their own purposes are but gradually revealed to them; they lack the mobility, the devices, and the ruthlessness of their opponents. This is a classical relationship in romances. The rationale of evil, being self-aggrandizing or destructive or both, is easily formulated and put into execution; evil has many devices and enjoys early success, seemingly to the point of being invincible. Good lacks this advantage. Its proponents are required to discriminate between what actually is and what only appears to be of the enemy. Within themselves they have few of the resources, militant and diplomatic, which evil can command. Good must rely on itself, its own faith and durability. It must work within a restrictive frame of justice and mercy; it may not, like evil, injure wantonly and conquer simply in accordance with desire. Hence the forces of good often suffer early defeat and hold out in peril until fortunes begin to change. The change may have any of several causes or all. Sometimes evil weakens itself and deteriorates with prosperity. More important, the faith and fortitude of the good exert against trial an energy which is intrinsic though not at first called forth. And this strength, once mobilized, increases with onslaughts against it. This capability can scarcely be distinguished from such supernatural or divine assistance as cannot fail to triumph. Prince Arthur of *The Faerie Queene* or the "thousand liveried angels" promised in *Comus* (though never needed) are always at hand, even if unseen. Sometimes these powers intervene; sometimes their presence only conveys strength to their favorites. Perhaps it makes little difference. What emerges is what was foreknown: that good, become virtue, must triumph, however formidable evil may seem.

Thus, in the romances of Williams there is no fundamental suspense. Rather there is what for many readers seems more gratifying—a temporary anxiety playing over a solid foundation of confidence. This anxiety may simulate genuine desperation when the forces of evil, in spectacular movement, seem invincible; conversely, when they are in rout, the punitive pleasures of confounding the enemy and the satisfaction in order re-established seem equal to those of a triumph which was really in doubt. Thus is generated an emotionalism which is like to be more facile *because* the possibility of irremediable disaster is never present. Some find in this a fraudulent appeal and exploitation, and liken the responses to those prompted by melodrama, whether of Pamela or Pauline or Sir Richard Hannay.

Whatever the judgment on this objection, Williams makes his narratives exciting. Excitement resides in the external events, provided usually by disruptive and often exotic forces invading familiar places and commonplace lives; Williams seemingly cared little for exotic settings. Excitement also resides in the choices which his characters must make. They do not have psychic and emotional conflicts but rather debates with self over their allegiances. These spiritual crises so engage them that the deep feeling of meditation and inquiry are conveyed to the reader. With external and internal events, Williams regularly builds his romances to breathless, climactic scenes in which awesome powers vent themselves and stupendous, though familiar, truths are revealed in explosions of enlightenment. Excitement in these scenes often overpowers clarity, but an engaged reader will have little difficulty at the time in forfeiting the value which he places on intellectual tidiness.

One more subject needs discussion in this review of the interaction of doctrine and method in Williams' fiction — his use of myth, both inherited and created. To this he doubtless had a personal disposition, increased by his wide, if somewhat disorderly, learning. Though no university man, Williams was a welcome member of the "Inklings," that group of Christian friends who for a time during World War II met regularly in Oxford to read and discuss their work in progress. It was a learned group — C. S. Lewis and his brother W. H. Lewis, a historian; J. R. R. Tolkien; H. V. D. Dyson; Nevill Coghill; and others. Lewis left testimony of his high personal regard for Williams. In the foreword to a collection of essays honoring his recently deceased friend, Lewis wrote, "No event has so corroborated my faith in the next world as Williams did simply by dying. When the idea of death and the idea of Williams thus met in my mind, it was the idea of death that was changed." [6] Earlier, in a letter to Dom Bede Griffiths, Lewis recorded the success of a lecture ("a panegyric of chastity") on *Comus*, which Williams delivered to the undergraduates. The lecture was a triumph of the indwelling spirit. Lewis wrote,

> He is an ugly man with rather a cockney voice. But no one ever thinks of this for 5 minutes after he has begun speaking. His face becomes almost angelic. But in public and in private he is of nearly all the men I have met, the one whose address most overflows with *love*. It is simply irresistible. These young men and women were lapping up what he said about Chastity before the end of the hour. It's a big thing to have done. [7]

Further along in the same letter some reservations appear:

> His stories . . . are his best work. *Descent into Hell* and *The Place of the Lion* are the best. I quite agree with you about what you call his "affectations"—not that they are affectations, but honest defects of taste. He is largely a self-educated man, labouring under an almost oriental richness of imagination ("Clotted glory from Charles" as Dyson called it) which could be saved from turning silly or even vulgar in print only by a severe early discipline which he never had. But he is a lovely creature. I'm proud of being among his friends.[8]

These extended quotations suggest why myth itself and a mythical way of narration attracted Williams and, even more, how his doctrinal purposes and his fictional method conform. From the bountiful discussions of the past twenty years, it is evident that myth is useful to those who have messages about which they feel some personal urgency. From C. S. Lewis's report, Williams felt deeply about chastity. I do not hesitate to infer also that he understood "the sage and serious doctrine of virginity," as Milton did. Personal engagement, knowledge of concept, and imagination combined to enable his delivering an effective address, a lay sermon, upon an ideal which has been so repeatedly urged in exhortation and illustrated in fiction that it is a continuing archetype of spiritual conduct. One may guess that Williams' discourse little resembled that paradigm of virtue rewarded by which Samuel Richardson perverted the doctrine for all posterity. For Williams, chastity was a virtue positive and dynamic, needing no reward. Regrettably for my purpose, he nowhere makes chastity a central theme in his prose fiction. It may be understood, however, that a number of his characters either obey or violate the prescription, usually more in fancy than in fact. Such a violator is Lawrence Wentworth in *Descent into Hell*, with his daydreams about "the almost Adela," a self-created Lilith-figure. What Williams brought off on the occasion which Lewis cites, is the characteristic on a larger scale of his romances.

Much of the substance of Williams' fiction derives from his adoption of the material, both detailed and general, of inherited mythology. Most prevalent is the Christian, but echoes of Neoplatonic, gypsy, Islamic, Arthurian also abound; the last named is much more prominent in his poetry. To the learned reader these give a pleasure of recognition. But the usefulness does not end here; Williams was not writing just for those who would —or might—compose exegetical notes. More important is the fact that he made mythical material his own by subjecting its original disparities to his own syncretizing, by adapting it to contemporary persons and circumstances, and by fusing narrative which is mythical in origin with narrative of his own invention.

Williams' adaptation of well-known myths provides somewhat the same cadre of knowledge that they provide in Greek tragedy. This possession further releases the reader from distracting doubts as to the outcome, and he is thus free to follow the means of realization and to be engaged by the partisan emotions which the narrative generates. The cadre aspect of the familiar has yet another effect. Doctrinally, Williams was an habitual syncretist; he was this also artistically. Into the associative framework of well-known myths Williams regularly fits pieces of recondite lore as well as incidents and symbols of his own making. Such is his skill in assembling and extending that he gains a double advantage: the unfamiliar material retains the charm of novelty while it is rendered intelligible and persuasive by its coalescence with the familiar.

For readers with a disposition to believe, the romances of Williams provide welcome assurances. Chief among these is a fortified confidence that right and order will prevail even against the gates of hell. Another is a vision of the ultimate unity of faiths and of stories which concern fundamental issues. Williams seems to have known that a desire to perceive unity, rather than fragmentation, is a strong motive in many minds and sensibilities, even in a time which has long been indoctrinated with the claims of analysis. Perhaps, indeed, the expositors of fragmentation have been so successful in spreading uneasiness that they have created a longing to believe in its opposite, a longing comforted by the romances of Charles Williams.

Charles Williams
The Fusions of Fiction

PATRICIA MEYER SPACKS

I enjoy reading Charles Williams. It's not like having a taste for heroin, but I make the confession in the defiant tone of Kingsley Amis admitting his predilection for science fiction. I can go for years without a Williams novel, but once I start one, I always finish. And I like Tolkien, which allies me with a generation of teen-agers, and C. S. Lewis, particularly his children's books, which may suggest yet greater regressiveness.

The literary critic in me, however, cannot fail to notice that Williams' work seems full of false notes, unable to justify its pretensions, lacking in imaginative energy, dependent on theological notions rather than fictional insights. Why, then, do I take pleasure in it? What is the relation between my compulsive, embarrassed reading of these novels and the judgment which damns them? Are my enjoyment and my disapproval both valid responses? To what, exactly, do they respond?

On one level, the pleasure of reading a Williams novel is like that of indulging in high class detective fiction or ghost stories: pure escapism, made more appealing if it touches on important issues. But Williams demands to be taken more seriously than this. The ultimate source of his appeal, it seems to me, is the extraordinary ambition of the attempt he makes: not merely to write good fiction, not just to dramatize theological issues, but to create a new twentieth-century form, an equivalent for the great medieval allegories. The attempt fails, but it suggests important issues in the fiction of our time.

For the medieval technique of attempting to fuse different levels of meaning—anagogical, topological, allegorical, literal—Williams substituted an effort to fuse different levels of experience: theological, supernatural, psychological. Medieval thinkers believed that the universe was structured analogically, that the intricacies of their literary patterns reflected the intricacies of reality. Williams appears to have believed much the same thing. Many Christian intellectuals have been aware that the psychological and the theological might reveal equivalent truths; Williams' special contribution was to bring the supernatural into close relation with them. The supernatural, in his novels, is a bridge between psychology and theology. It provides objective correlatives for modes of feeling: a sense of the menace of the universe and the dangers of self-knowledge (the doppelgänger in *Descent into Hell*), malice and power-lust (the Snake and the Lion of *The Place of the Lion*), emotional conviction of the enduring force of art (the supernaturally long life of Nigel Considine in *Shadows of Ecstasy*). But the same images objectify theological truths. The doppelgänger means also the joy of accepted responsibility for one's freedom, the Lion and the Snake are emblems of divine energy, Considine's longevity signifies his sinful rejection of the human condition. Often—as in the examples given—the moral weight attached to the theological meaning contradicts that of the psychological meaning: Pauline's doppelgänger, a psychological evil, becomes a theological good. There are also simpler cases: Evelyn's rejection of others in *All Hallows' Eve* becomes rejection of God, Wentworth's psychological self-obsession in *Descent into Hell* turns diabolical. Such paradoxes of value help to establish the ambiguities of perception, the need to be capable of faith beyond perception.

Neither Tolkien nor Lewis is ambitious in this particular way. Tolkien reduces psychological concern to a minimum, involving his readers in a pattern of events and the meaning of that pattern; Lewis in his adult theological novels subordinates psychology to theology except in a few sketchy instances (for example, the characterization of

Mark Studdock and of his wife in *That Hideous Strength*); in his children's books he commits himself to allegory. Williams, in his effort to achieve significant fusion, invites comparison with the imaginative theological writers of the past: Milton, Dante. But any attempt at such comparison seems forced because Williams' work so conspicuously lacks grandeur and true cosmic scope.

Cosmic scope is not easy to come by. Eighteenth-century critics pointed out that poets could no longer use the pagan mythology which gave richness to classic epics because popular belief did not support it; it would seem mere decoration; Christian "machinery" should substitute for it. The attrition of belief continues; a work which employed the Christian mythology of heaven and hell in literal or pseudo-literal terms would now appear outmoded, suspect, irrelevant. Lewis solved the problem ingeniously by using the contemporary tradition of science fiction to evoke other worlds; Tolkien evaded it by creating a universe without a deity, by dealing with morals rather than theology, and by depending on geographic rather than cosmic immensities. Williams reminds us of the cosmos within; he relies on complexity instead of grandeur. The supernatural phenomena which abound in his novels hint the connections between the unfathomable depths of the personality and the mysteries of the larger universe, but there is no systematic cosmology. The City, emblem of man's community with God, recurs as a symbolic reference; its nature, however, is never specified.

To accept complexity as a substitute for cosmic range accords with the modern temper, yet Williams' novels have not generated wide enthusiasm: they remain the property of a cult. One reason may be that their complexity dissolves upon close examination because the fusion attempted seems finally inconceivable. The theological realizations of the novels subsume so much that they make psychological complexity (and consequently psychological realism) impossible. Theological insight is always in some sense complex; but in another, simple. Its special quality is finality: once achieved, it solves problems; no amount of verbal manipulation can convince one that the problems remain. Other problems emerge, but in a theological framework only salvation matters. Once Pauline realizes that it is possible for men to bear one another's burdens, once she entrusts her fear to Peter Stanhope, the reader cannot await with real tension the next appearance of her double: as a problem, the double no longer exists. Conversely, Lawrence Wentworth's commitment to the path of damnation is apparent early in *Descent into Hell*. One feels some interest in how his damnation is to be fulfilled, and in what will happen when Pauline meets her double, but the interest is more intellectual than emotional.

In his study of science fiction, *New Maps of Hell* (a title which suggests the affinities between scientific and theological fiction), Kingsley Amis quotes Edmund Crispin on characterization: "The characters in a science fiction story are usually treated rather as representatives of their species than as individuals in their own right. They are matchstick men and matchstick women, for the reason that if they were not, the anthropocentric habit of our culture would cause us, in reading, to give altogether too much attention to them and altogether too little to the non-human forces which constitute the important remainder of the *dramatis personae*." A bit later, Mr. Amis suggests that "idea as hero" is the foundation of much science fiction: it "occupies the position given in ordinary fiction to matters of human situation or character." These are strangely old-fashioned concepts to dominate so modern a form. They recall Dr. Johnson's theory and practice in *Rasselas*, another work in which idea is the hero and matchstick characters call our attention to forces beyond themselves, a work which reminds us that the concern of the writer is not to number the streaks on the tulip but to reveal general truths beyond the particular. Such is Charles Williams' concern, although his apparent interest in psychology disguises it. Like the science fictionist and the classicist, he directs us toward important truths. His fiction seems more immediate than Johnson's, more broadly relevant than Isaac Asimov's, because psychological trimmings obscure its theoretical foundation. But since they are only trimmings they cannot fully engage us; they do not appear really to have engaged their creator.

Corresponding difficulties emerge when we examine the second element in Williams' triad of concerns, his supernatural material. For his psychological preoccupation, insofar as it is convincing, he has the support of a century's novelistic tradition which prepares his readers to interest themselves in minutiae of impulse and compulsion. The most successful fiction of our time has involved us in its characters' psyches; when Williams reveals the mind of a strange person under strange stresses—Betty's mother, for instance, in *All Hallows' Eve*—we are ready to be interested, although we may be disappointed in the long run to discover that the psychological problems are pseudo-problems, only the theological ones real. Supernatural subjects, on the other hand, belong to the tradition of sensational fiction. Their serious literary employment has been minimal; they suggest that an author values effect more than meaning. They bring up the problem of belief in a new and acute form. Readers willing to accept the idea of Williams' kind of fusion are likely to have difficulty with this aspect of it. For one thing, Williams' use of the supernatural often evades real problems. Chloe Burnett, in *Many Dimensions*, awakes to find a midnight intruder in her room. She makes her will perfect; the intruder is struck dead. Simon the Clerk (*All Hallows' Eve*) needs a messenger. He creates the form of a woman out of dust and animates it with the spirits of the dead. Everything becomes easy; a *deus* (or *diabolus*) *ex machina* is always available. A mumbo-jumbo atmosphere clouds Williams' purpose; we may suspect him of frivolity, or of self-indulgence.

Yet his use of the supernatural is crucial to his intent. We must take our experience seriously, Williams argues; we can only do so by understanding what it is. The trivial may be important: a scholar who refuses to worry about the historical accuracy of actors' shoulder knots thus confirms his own damnation. But the sensational and improbable may be equally real and important. If we perceived the universe rightly, we would see how many of its phenomena exceed the possibility of our comprehension. Williams' wise characters—Pauline's grandmother and Peter Stanhope in *Descent into Hell*, for example, or Sibyl in *The Greater Trumps*—all understand that the supernatural is only an aspect of the natural. It may violate normal expectation, but it would be dangerous to disbelieve for that reason, to make human comprehension the standard for judging omnipotence. Williams' attempt at literary fusion dramatizes his belief that the universe operates through equivalent fusions; human perception may be unable to grasp them, but faith maintains their reality. Modern skepticism, these novels hint, may reflect narrow-mindedness rather than liberalism.

One can respect such ideas while remaining skeptical about the possibility of their convincing literary embodiment. The opening chapters of Williams' novels are usually compelling. The first encounter with the Lion in *The Place of the Lion*; Lester's gradual realization, in *All Hallows' Eve*, that she has become a member of the Wasteland's "unreal city," where death has undone so many; the quiet revelation that Pauline sometimes sees herself coming down the street (*Descent into Hell*) — these episodes or patterns have force and immediacy. The reader does not yet "know" the characters; he accepts on faith what the author chooses to tell him about them or to keep hidden. He does not trouble himself at first about the meaning of the narrative's remarkable events. Their immediate justification is their fictional interest. Although Williams' often portentous tone hints that larger issues are at stake, he functions initially as a story-teller, exploiting the appeal of the mysterious.

But it soon becomes necessary to assert meanings which the symbolic events and objects do not naturally embody. Demonstrated meanings are often convincing; asserted meanings rarely so. The kinds of meanings that interest

Williams are not capable of demonstration. Over and over the novelist faces the sort of problem that Eliot dealt with in *Murder in the Cathedral*: how does one demonstrate the invisible descent of grace? Eliot shows us Thomas à Becket before and after he has been saved; our sense of the difference between the two states must support our understanding of what grace means. Williams, working in a less restrictive form, is free to state his meaning; his tone becomes disagreeable as he insists on the importance of what he tells us:

> The shape of Lawrence Wentworth's desire had emerged from the power of his body. He had assented to that making, and again, outside the garden of satisfied dreams, he had assented to the company of the shape which could not be except by his will and was imperceptibly to possess his will. Image without incarnation, it was the delight of his incarnation, for it was without any of the things that troubled him in the incarnation of the beloved. He could exercise upon it all arts but one; he could not ever discover by it or practise towards it the freedom of love. A man cannot love himself; he can only idolize it, and over the idol delightfully tyrannize—without purpose. The great gift which this simple idolatry of self gives is lack of further purpose; it is, the saints tell us, a somewhat similar thing that exists in those wholly possessed by their End; it is, human experience shows, the most exquisite delight in the interchanges of romantic love. But in all loves but one there are counterpointing times of purposes; in this only there are none.

This is not the language of the novelist; it is hard to believe that it is the language of a man steeped in English literature. Pedagogical, insistent, pretentious, it dissipates the reader's sense of the horror of Wentworth's succubus, makes him feel that the event only provides a pretext for the sermon. Vague ideas seem to mean more to the author than the concrete realities of his fiction. A garden cannot be just a garden, it must be asserted to be what it is not felt to be, a symbol: the garden of satisfied dreams. Abstractions multiply: *will, incarnation, delight, freedom, purpose.* The imprecise use of *thing* ("the things that troubled him," "a somewhat similar thing") reflects a vagueness of conception which makes the passage as unconvincing a sermon as it is a scene. The author does not take the supernatural event as seriously as he claims to; he only takes its meaning seriously, and he feels that meaning more than he understands it. His fusion seems finally unreal.

The false lyricism of the paragraph from *Descent into Hell* strikes a characteristic note. Sudden ascents of tone signal moments of importance in Williams' novels: "At last the awful change was done. She stood before him; her hands, still outstretched, were empty, but within her and about her light as of a lovely and clearer day grew and expanded. No violent outbreak or dazzling splendour was there; a perfection of existence flowed from her and passed outward so that he seemed both to stand in it and to look on it with his natural eyes. With such eyes he saw also, black upon her forehead, as if the night corresponding to that new day dwelled there for a while apart, the letters of the Tetragrammaton." That is from *Many Dimensions*, first published in 1931, but all the later novels contain equivalent passages. They attempt to deal with the supernatural in the context of realistic fiction by rising above the restrictions of realism to the Biblical-poetic. But the vagueness of mysticism ("a perfection of existence flowed from her") defeats the attempt. Williams needs images like Dante's, rich, self-defining, supported by linguistic power. He does not have them at his command.

The enormous philosophic and technical problems of writing fiction in the twentieth century increase when an author's purposes are theological as well as imaginative. The traditional concern of fiction has been the intersection of the individual with his society. In our time this often means man in rebellion against society, trying to escape or to defy; but as the novel moves toward a preoccupation with man in the universe, it moves toward the techniques of lyric poetry. Williams' concern with man in his cosmic relations is central in his fiction; he faces the difficulty of turning abstract perceptions into recognizable experience. He takes none of the easy ways out: he does not retreat into the historic or mythic past, he does not create new worlds for his characters or in fact achieve true lyricism. Instead he tries to employ the conventions of the realistic novel, to convey the outlines of a social world inhabited by recognizable human beings and yet to serve more than realistic purposes. In his most compelling moments, he makes experience seem both plausible and reverberant with uncanny significance: the discovery of the corpse under the desk in *War in Heaven*, his first novel, is a striking case in point.

The most successful theological fiction of the twentieth century—in English, the work of such writers as Graham Greene, Muriel Spark, Iris Murdoch comes to mind—has limited itself to realistic conventions. None of the events in these novelists' works remain inexplicable. Although the bizarre becomes the commonplace in much of Miss Murdoch's fiction, which is rich in incest, violence, depravity, the supernatural is on the whole excluded. Greene, Miss Murdoch, Miss Spark at their best write philosophic fiction. They report events for which psychological explanations might seem adequate and make us see in them meanings beyond the psychological, patterns which suggest large truths. The fictional integrity of their novels remains inviolate; it leads to a more significant philosophic integrity.

Charles Williams, reaching for more than they, achieves less. The attempt to fuse different levels of experience which dominates his novels is fundamentally allegorical, but he cannot commit himself to the limitations of allegory. His introduction of supernatural phenomena and events indicates also his impatience with realistic convention: he wishes to tell us that we must expand our conceptions of what realism is. Since what he wishes to say seems more important to him than how he says it, he sacrifices the imaginative life of his novels to purposes which are didactic rather than philosophic. The little sermons which keep intruding into his fiction suggest his greater concern with ends than with means; he is unable to confine himself to the structure of the realistic novel.

Critics have been tempted to find allegorical meanings in the fiction of Lewis and Tolkien as well as Williams. None of the books quite submits to allegorical interpretation; all seem to invite it. And none quite communicates as much meaning as it seems to intend. In Lewis's seven books for children, he embarked on systematic allegory; the result, it seems to me, was more successful than any of his adult fiction. His aim and his style in the Narnia books were modest in comparison with Tolkien's or Williams', but his aim was richly achieved: one is left with no residual uneasiness. But uneasiness remains after reading a Williams novel. The author cannot sustain the unification of experience and of sensibility that he attempts. At his best, near allegory, he attains great symbolic richness, but he cannot sustain that either; the temptation to didacticism overwhelms him. Williams' ideas are compelling and so is his fictional purpose, his attempt to unite what in experience seems disparate. In the early chapters of his novels, before one feels the full demands of realistic conventions, and at isolated moments later, he achieves his ambitious fusion. Finally, though, his aims exceed his literary ability. The fusion splits, one feels the novelist manipulating, hears the theologian exhorting, realizes how superior medieval methods are to this version of twentieth-century ones for conveying the subtleties of theology in imaginative form.

Notes

WALSH—C. S. Lewis

1. Ed. Jocelyn Gibb (New York, 1966).
2. Ed., with a Memoir, W. H. Lewis (New York, 1966).

HALDANE—Auld Hornie, F.R.S.

1. *On Hegel's Philosophy of Law* (1844).

PLANK—Some Psychological Aspects

1. In references from here on out abridged as *O, P, T*. Page numbers refer to the following editions: *O*—New York: Avon, #Y-127, *P*—New York: Macmillan, 1944. *T*—London: Pan Books, #X 266, 1955. We have two versions of *That Hideous Strength*: the original (1945) and an abridged one (1955). The latter seems to me the better book. This sounds strange, as we generally think of later modification as only rust and ruin; but a book may have a sort of life of its own once it has been given birth, and rust and ruin are not always unkind. There are buildings on which a spark of the divine seems to have descended after they lost their original splendor; examples come to mind, from Cape Sounion to Heidelberg Castle. And, would the sight of the Venus of Milo be as overwhelming if she still had her arms?

2. "Psychoanalysis and Literary Criticism" in N. C. Smith, ed., *Essays and Studies by Members of the English Association*, XVII (1941), 7–21.

3. Cf. Jessie L. Weston, *From Ritual to Romance* (Cambridge, 1920).

4. Especially in lines 424–26: "I sat upon the shore / Fishing, with the arid plain behind me / Shall I at least set my land in order?" I had failed to notice these connections; the editor of this volume drew my attention to them. Perhaps I should be ashamed so to confess my igno-

rance, but Lewis had anticipated that much: the effectiveness of the scene where Jane Studdock is introduced to "Mr. Fisher-King" depends on her *not* being aware of the meaning of the name—and she is a graduate student of English, working on a doctoral thesis on Donne!

5. Charles Williams, *Descent into Hell* (New York, 1949).

6. G. Barag, "Zur Psychoanalyse der Prostitution," *Imago*, XXIII (1937), 330–62.

7. In a radio talk in 1960, for instance, he referred to the trilogy as "my three science fiction books" (*Of Other Worlds* [London, 1966], p. 42).

8. In his "Memoir of C. S. Lewis," published as Introduction to *Letters of C. S. Lewis* (London, 1966).

9. R. P. Marsh, "Meaning and the Mind-Drugs," *ETC.: A Review of General Semantics*, XXII (1965) (Special Issue on the Psychedelic Experience), 408–25.

10. R. E. L. Masters, and J. Houston, *The Varieties of Psychedelic Experience* (New York, 1966), p. 106.

11. *Ibid.*, p. 152.

12. A. Huxley, *The Doors of Perception* (New York, 1954), p. 16.

HILLEGAS—*Out of The Silent Planet* as Cosmic Voyage

1. Thorough explication of Lewis's use of myth can be found, for example, in Wayne Shumaker, "The Cosmic Trilogy of C. S. Lewis," *Hudson Review*, VIII (Summer, 1955), 240–54, and Charles Moorman, *Arthurian Triptych* (Berkeley and Los Angeles, 1960), pp. 102–26.

2. "Lighter than Air, But Heavy as Hate," *Partisan Review*, XXIV (Winter, 1957), 109.

3. *Of Other Worlds* (London, 1966), p. 12.

4. In a letter to an unknown correspondent, quoted in Roger Lancelyn Green, *C. S. Lewis* (New York, 1963), p. 26. Lewis offers some very perceptive comments on *The First Men in the Moon*, particularly the chapter, "Mr. Bedford Alone," in "On Stories." His observations in the same essay on the idea of "extraterrestrial" in *The War of the Worlds* are also valuable.

5. New York, 1944, prefatory note. All subsequent references are to this edition, which was published by Macmillan.

6. *Seven Science Fiction Novels of H. G. Wells* (New York, 1950), p. 485.

7. *Ibid.*, p. 486.

8. *Of Other Worlds*, p. 12.

9. C. S. Lewis, *Letters* (London, 1966), p. 205.

10. *Of Other Worlds*, p. 69.

11. Robert Conquest, "The Art of the Enemy," *Essays in Criticism*, VII (January, 1957), 42–55. See also my discussion in *The Future as Nightmare: H. G. Wells and the Anti-Utopians* (New York, 1967), pp. 133–44, of Lewis's attack in the trilogy on the Wells-Stapledon-Haldane ideas.

MOORMAN—The Fictive Worlds of C. S. Lewis and J. R. R. Tolkien

1. Originally published in *Essays Presented to Charles Williams* (London, 1947) and reprinted in a revised version in *The Tolkien Reader* (New York, 1966).

2. Charles Moorman, *The Precincts of Felicity: The Augustinian City of the Oxford Christians* (Gainesville, 1966), p. 96.

3. ". . . And Telling You a Story," *Essays Presented to Charles Williams*, p. 10.

4. "On Stories," *Essays Presented to Charles Williams*, p. 103.

5. *The Portable Faulkner*, ed. Malcolm Cowley (New York, 1946), p. 5.

6. *The Lord of the Rings* is published in three volumes—*The Fellowship of the Ring* (1954), *The Two Towers* (1954), and *The Return of the King* (1955)—by George Allen and Unwin in London. For the sake of convenience I have designated the three volumes by the numerals I, II, and III rather than by their proper titles in referring to them in my text.

7. *The Lion, the Witch and the Wardrobe* (London, 1950), p. 20.

8. J. R. R. Tolkien, "Beowulf: The Monsters and the Critics," *Proceedings of the British Academy*, XXII (1936), 295.

KILBY—Meaning in *The Lord of the Rings*

1. *The Fellowship of the Ring* (London, 1954), pp. 246–49.

2. *Ibid.*, pp. 245–46.

3. Such books as *Poetic Diction* (London, 1952), *History in English Words* (1954), and *Saving the Appearances* (London, 1957).

4. Preface to D. E. Harding's *The Hierarchy of Heaven and Earth* (London, 1952).

5. *Tree and Leaf* (London, 1964), pp. 51–52. A boy, says C. S. Lewis, "does not despise real woods because he has read of enchanted woods: the reading makes all real woods a little enchanted." *Of Other Worlds* (London, 1966), pp. 29–30.

6. *Tree and Leaf*, p. 53.

7. *Ibid.*, p. 55.

8. "History often resembles 'Myth,'" says Tolkien, "because they are both ultimately of the same stuff." *Tree and Leaf*, p. 31.

9. "The Cosmic Kingdom of Myth," unpubl. Ph.D. diss. (University of Illinois, 1960).

10. *The Two Towers*, pp. 338–39 and C. S. Lewis, *That Hideous Strength* (Macmillan, 1947), p. 265. Note: I have frequently mentioned Lewis and Tolkien together because, as is generally known, they were close friends and critics at Oxford who frequently read their manuscripts to one another for criticism.

11. *An Experiment in Criticism* (Cambridge, Eng.), p. 67.

12. *Angles and Britons* (Cardiff, Wales, 1963), pp. 40–41.

13. *The Return of the King* (London, 1955), p. 232.

14. New York *Times Book Review*, October 31, 1954, p. 37.

HUGHES—Pieties and Giant Forms in *The Lord of the Rings*

1. Available most easily in *The Tolkien Reader* (New York, 1966).

2. *Biographia Literaria*, ed. J. Shawcross (Oxford, 1907), II, 12. My italics.

3. *Coleridge's Essays and Lectures on Shakespeare* (London, 1911), p. 66.

4. *Waiting for God* (New York, 1951), p. 126.

5. *Ibid.*, p. 145.

6. *The Unmediated Vision* (New York, 1966), p. 128.

URANG—Tolkien's Fantasy

1. J. R. R. Tolkien, "On Fairy-Stories," in *Essays Presented to Charles Williams* (London, 1947), p. 70.

2. Page references (by volume and page, in parentheses: e.g. II, 244) will be to the Houghton Mifflin edition (1956): Vol. I, *The Fellowship of the Ring*; Vol. II, *The Two Towers*; Vol. III, *The Return of the King*.

3. Tolkien, "On Fairy-Stories," pp. 42, 62.

4. C. S. Lewis, "The Gods Return to Earth," *Time and Tide*, Aug. 14, 1954, 1083.

5. Northrop Frye, *Anatomy of Criticism* (Princeton, 1957), pp. 186–87.

6. Tolkien, "On Fairy-Stories," p. 53.

7. William Blissett, "Despots of the Rings," *South Atlantic Quarterly*, LVII (Summer, 1959), 153–54.

8. J. V. Langmead Casserley, *Toward a Theology of History* (London, 1965), p. 92.

9. H. H. Rowley, *The Relevance of Apocalyptic* (London, 1944), p. 32.

10. Tolkien, "On Fairy-Stories," pp. 81–83.

11. J. R. R. Tolkien, "Beowulf: The Monsters and the Critics," from *Proceedings of the British Academy*, XXII (1936), 286.

12. C. S. Lewis, *English Literature in the Sixteenth Century, Excluding Drama* (London, 1954), p. 342.

13. C. S. Lewis, *Rehabilitations and Other Essays* (London, 1939), p. 29.

14. Lewis, "The Gods Return to Earth," p. 1082.

15. Tolkien, "Beowulf: The Monsters and the Critics," pp. 256–7.

16. Casserley, p. 222.

17. Edmund Wilson, "Oo, Those Awful Orcs!" *Nation*, April 14, 1956, 314.

WINSHIP—The Novels of Charles Williams

1. Mary McDermott Shideler, *The Theology of Romantic Love* (Grand Rapids, 1966), p. 4; and Alice Mary Hadfield, *An Introduction to Charles Williams* (London, 1959), p. 76.

2. The novels are cited from Faber and Faber editions except as noted. In order of composition they are as follows, with dates of first publication and of the cited editions: *Shadows of Ecstasy* (written in the 1920's), 1931, 1948; *War in Heaven*, 1930, 1949; *Many Dimensions*, 1931, 1947; *The Place of the Lion* (Gollancz), 1931, 1947; *The Greater Trumps*, 1932, 1954; *Descent into Hell* (written about 1933), 1937, 1949; *All Hallows' Eve*, 1945, 1945.

3. See, for example, Hadfield, p. 79.

4. New York, 1959, p. 310. First published in 1941.

5. *Arthurian Torso* (London, 1948), p. 123.

IRWIN—Christian Doctrine and the Tactics of Romance

1. T. S. Eliot, Introduction to Charles Williams, *All Hallows' Eve* (New York, 1948), p. xiii.

2. *Descent into Hell* (New York, 1949), p. 211.

3. "This Rough Magic: The Novels of Charles Williams," *Yale Review*, NS XL (Winter, 1951), 290.

4. *Anatomy of Criticism* (Princeton, 1957), pp. 304–5.

5. Eliot, p. xvi.

6. *Essays Presented to Charles Williams* (London, 1947), p. xiv.

7. *Letters of C. S. Lewis*, ed. W. H. Lewis (New York, 1966), pp. 196–97 (to Dom Bede Griffiths, O.S.B., 21 December 1941). See also p. 177 (to W. H. Lewis, 11 February 1940).

8. *Ibid.*, p. 197.

Index

Adonais, 83
Amis, Kingsley, xvi, 150
Ariosto, Lodovico, 43
Arnim, Ludwig Achim von, 31
Asimov, Isaac, 154
Atlas Shrugged, 112
Auden, W. H., 80
Auf zwei Planeten, 51

Barag, G., 161*n*
Barfield, Owen, 7, 8–9, 31, 71
Barth, John, xiii
Beowulf, 62, 64, 68
Biographia Literaria, 82
"Black Pits of Luna, The," 45
Blake, William, 93, 95
Blissett, William, 102
Brave New World, xiii, 124
Burroughs, Edgar Rice, xiii

Casserley, J. V. Langmead, 109
Coghill, Nevill, 8, 146
Coleridge, Samuel Taylor, 82, 84
Collins, Wilkie, 5
Comus, 145
Conquest, Robert, 58
Cosmic voyage, 42–46
Crispin, Edmund, 153
Cyrano de Bergerac, 43

David Copperfield, 85
Davies, Sir John, 114
Derleth, August, xiv
Detective story, 112
Dickens, Charles, 96
Divine Comedy, xiii
Dyson, H. V. D., 146

Eddison, E. R., xiv
Eliot, T. S., xv, xvi, 28, 114, 130, 141, 144, 156
Eyers, Harold, 130

Faerie Queene, 145
Fantasy, xiii–xv
Faust, xiii
Fielding, Henry, 143
First Men in the Moon, The, xv, 42, 44, 45, 46–49 *passim*, 55
Flaubert, Gustave, 35
Food of the Gods, The, 19
Forster, E. M., 112
From the Earth to the Moon and Round the Moon, 44
Frye, Northrop, 100, 101, 142

Ghost story, 124
Gibb, Jocelyn, 160*n*
Gillispie, C. C., xvi
Godwin, Francis, 43
Golem fantasy, 31–33
Gormenghast Trilogy, xiv, xviii

Gothic novel, xv, 112
Green, Roger Lancelyn, 161n
Greene, Graham, 158
Gresham, Joy Davidman, 2, 11–12
Gulliver's Travels, 58

Hadfield, Alice Mary, 164n
Hartmann, Geoffrey H., 95
Heinlein, Robert, 45
Hopkins, Gerard Manley, 89
Houston, J., 161n
Huxley, Aldous, xiii, 161n
Hymn to the Sun, 31

Ikhnaton, 31
"Inklings," 146
Isabella in Aegypten, 31

James, Henry, 112
Jerusalem, 95
Johnson, Samuel, 11, 153, 154

Kafka, Franz, xiii, 35–36, 49
Kepler, Johann, 42, 43

Lasswitz, Kurd, 51
Lawlor, John, 7
Lewis, C. S.: xiii–xviii, 1–69, 71, 106, 111, 146; public image and private reality, 1–3, 7–11; logic and romance, 3–4; antimodernism, 4–7; attitude toward science, 17–19; fantasies about "Animal Land," 37; concept of myth, 75–76; on Charles Williams, 121, 146–47;
—The Allegory of Love, 13; Christian Behaviour, 23; Chronicles of Narnia, xv, 1, 13, 59–62, 66–68, 69, 159; An Experiment in Criticism, 163n; The Four Loves, 12; "The Gods Return to Earth," 164n; The Great Divorce, 4, 13, 20, 21; A Grief Observed, 12, 13; "The Inner Ring," 3; Letters, 2, 8; Mere Christianity, 12, 13; "On Science Fiction," 49–50; "On Stories," 45–46, 49, 61; Open Letter to Dr. Tillyard, 8; Out of the Silent Planet, xv, 1, 15–58 passim; Perelandra, xiv, xv, 1, 15–40 passim, 41, 42; Reflections on the Psalms, 31; "Sometimes Fairy Stories May Say Best What's to be Said," 59–60; Surprised by Joy, 2, 3, 36; That Hideous Strength, xv, 1, 2–3, 15–40, 41, 42, 67, 76, 152; Till We Have Faces, xv, 1, 11, 13
Lewis, W. H., 2, 3, 37, 146
Light on C. S. Lewis, 2, 7, 38
Lindsay, David, xiv, 49
Lovecraft, H. P., xiv
Lowell, Percival, 50–51
Lucian of Samosata, 43
Lyrical Ballads, 82

Macdonald, George, 4, 6
Magic Mountain, The, 112
Man in the Moone, 43
Marsh, R. P., 161n
Martian myth, 50–51, 112
Marx, Karl, 20
Masters, R. E. L., 161n
Metamorphosis, xiii
Mind Parasites, The, xiv
Moorman, Charles, 161n, 162n
Murder in the Cathedral, 156

Murders in the Rue Morgue, 112

Murdoch, Iris, xiii, 158

Nabokov, Vladimir, xiii
New Maps of Hell, xvi–xvii, 153
Nibelungenlied, 68
Nicholson, Daniel, 130
Nicolson, Marjorie, 42, 46, 49
Nineteen Eighty-four, xiii, 124
Nottingham, Ernest, 130

Odyssey, xiii
Once and Future King, The, 82
Orchestra, 114
Orlando Furioso, 43
Orwell, George, xiii

Pamela, 112
Paradise Lost, xiii, 41
Parker, Douglass, xv
Peake, Merwyn, xiv
Phantastes, 4
Plank, Robert, 45
Poe, Edgar Allan, 44
"Pure Representation," 95

Rabelais, François, 43
Rowley, H. H., 105

St. Julien l'Hôpitalier, 35
Sayers, Dorothy, 61
Scholes, Robert, xiii
Science fiction, xv, 19–20, 33–34, 49, 152, 153–54
Shaftesbury, Anthony Ashley Cooper, Earl of, 81
Shelley, Percy Bysshe, 81, 83
Shideler, Mary McDermott, 111
Shumaker, Wayne, 161*n*
Somnium, 42

Song of Roland, The, 62
Spark, Muriel, 158
Stapledon, William Olaf, 19

Tarot pack, 114, 119
Teilhard de Chardin, Pierre, 6
Tempest, The, 84
Tolkien, J. R. R.: xiii–xviii, 59–110, 146, 159; concept of myth, 75–76; sense of humor, 77–78; phonological gift, 78–80; concept of fantasy, 81–83, 97–101 *passim*
—"Beowulf: The Monsters and the Critics," 74, 106–8; *Farmer Giles of Ham,* 77, 79; *The Hobbit,* 77, 83, 84, 87; "Leaf by Niggle," 77; *The Lord of the Rings,* xiv, xv, 59–66, 67, 68, 69, 70–80, 81–96, 97–110; "On Fairy-Stories," 59, 61, 63, 81, 96, 101; *Tree and Leaf,* 75
Tom Jones, 112
Trial, The, 64
True History, 43
Tucker, George, 44
Turn of the Screw, The, 124

"Unparalleled Adventures of One Hans Pfaal, The," 44

Verne, Jules, 44, 45
Virginian, The, 112
A Voyage to Arcturus, xiv, 49
A Voyage to the Moon, 44
Voyages to the Moon, 42
Voyages to the Sun and Moon, 43

War of the Worlds, The, 51, 55
Warren, Austin, 43

Waste Land, The, 28, 114, 122

We, xiii

Weil, Simone, 83, 85, 89

Weird Tales, xiv

Wellek, René, 43

Welles, Orson, 51

Wells, H. G., xiv, 19, 42, 44, 45, 51, 55, 58

Weston, Jessie L., 160*n*

White, T. H., 82

Williams, Charles: xiii–xviii, 42, 58, 111–59; use of supernatural, 114–18, 154–59; role of correspondences, 119–20; doctrine of co-inherence, 120–22, 141–42; problem of power, 140–41; use of myth, 148

—*All Hallows' Eve,* xiv, 114–15, 120, 125, 127, 135, 136, 137, 140–41, 151, 154, 155; *Thomas Cranmer of Canterbury,* 132; *Death of Good Fortune,* 132; *Descent into Hell,* 32, 117–18, 120, 122, 124, 125, 128, 130, 131, 132, 134, 135, 136, 137, 142, 147, 151, 153, 155, 157; *The Figure of Arthur,* 138; *The Greater Trumps,* 113–14, 119, 124, 126, 127, 130,

133, 140, 155; *The House by the Stable,* 132; *The House of the Octopus,* 132; *Judgment at Chelmsford,* 132; *Many Dimensions,* 115, 120, 127, 129, 133, 136, 137, 140, 143, 144, 154, 157; *Masques,* 132; *The Place of the Lion,* 113, 122–23, 125, 126, 127–28, 131, 133, 134, 147, 151, 155; *Poems of Conformity,* 130; *The Region of the Summer Stars,* 135, 138; *Seed of Adam,* 132; *Shadows of Ecstasy,* 112, 113, 126, 127, 129, 131, 132, 134, 136, 137, 140, 151; *War in Heaven,* 112, 114, 115, 116, 126, 128, 129, 130, 131, 134, 140, 143, 158; *Witchcraft,* 116

Wilson, Colin, xiv

Wilson, Edmund, 110

Winship, George P., Jr., 142

Woman in White, The, 5

Wordsworth, William, 88, 95, 96

Worm Ouroboros, The, vix, xviii

Wright, Marjorie, 76

Zamyatin, Evgenii, xiii